Pugh Proverbs

Dwane Pugh

ISBN 978-1-63874-620-1 (paperback)
ISBN 978-1-63874-621-8 (digital)

Christian Faith Publishing, Inc.
832 Park Avenue
Meadville, PA 16335
www.christianfaithpublishing.com

Printed in the United States of America

To the glory of God,
with thanksgiving for the people who have
helped make this book possible

Pugh proverb: "Faith is tapping into the sovereignty of God and living it in the moment."

Scripture verses: Hebrews 11:1–40; James 2:14-26; Matthew 17:20; 1 Peter 1:7; Proverbs 3:5, 6

Have you ever seen a miracle? Maybe you don't believe in miracles. If you have never seen one, I can understand how you might come to the conclusion they don't exist. However, my life has been filled with so many miracles, I would be a fool not to acknowledge their existence.

As a child, I had always wanted to see a miracle with my own two eyes. I remember sitting on my mother's lap at bedtime as she read Bible stories to me. My eyes would widen, glistening with excitement as she told of the great exploits of the heroes of the Bible. My mother had a way of telling the stories that made me feel as if I was right there beside the characters as they stood for God in the face of impossible situations. Through my vivid imagination, I had been with David as he faced Goliath, and I climbed Mt. Sinai with Moses to behold the glory of God, talking with Him as friend with friend.

I also saw Jesus heal the sick, raise the dead, and preach the good news of the kingdom to those held captive by sin. My eyes would grow heavy, and I would lay down with Daniel on the soft fur of a lion and fall fast asleep. Little did I know that God had planned in my future a miracle of my own.

It was the summer of 1987. I, along with a group of four adults and nine teenagers, was going to visit one of our missionaries who

ministered in Mexico. As I worked hard on the necessary prepara-
tions, the Lord stirred my soul to start praying that the power of
Satan might be clearly seen and the power of the Lord to defeat Satan
be just as clear.

For too many times, my Christianity can lapse into a religious
ritual, "having a form of godliness but denying the power thereof"
(2 Timothy 3:5). I would then serve a God of my own perception,
putting God into the limited boundaries of what I think and feel He
is instead of falling down and worshipping Him that He may reveal
to me more of His limitless beauty and holiness. My mind's eye can
see God too small, and He was about to open them up to see the
reality of who He is.

In Mexico, my group was asked to hold a special service in the
middle of one of the villages that the missionaries were trying to
reach with the gospel. The homes looked like something out of a
John Wayne Western movie. They were a little more than logs and
sticks woven together with thatched roofs and Mexican blankets for
windows and doors. We went door to door, armed with a few phrases
in Spanish that invited the people to attend the service we were holding at their meeting place. The village met in a dirt area at its center,
worn down by the traffic of feet over the years.

As the villagers began to assemble, a missionary played music
on her accordion. It was a beautiful sunny day, and we were expecting a good crowd. After everyone arrived, we began the service of my
group by singing a couple of songs in Spanish. As we took our place,
right before we began to sing, one of my teenage girls' eyes rolled
back in her head and she fell flat on the ground. Her head made the
thudding sound of a ripe watermelon as it hit the dirt.

As if on cue, the wind began to whip around us as an ominous
black cloud came over the mountain range at the edge of the plateau.
A few drops of rain began to fall, adding to the disruption of the
moment. One of the men from our group took care of the fallen girl
as we tried to go on with the service. After our singing, I and a few
members of our group stood behind the villagers, discussing in whis-
pers what to do if the rain should come.

I looked over the crowd to see a restlessness setting in. I turned to my friends and said, "God's not going to let it rain on us. Pray!" I got alone under a nearby tree and earnestly sought God to do for me what I had been told He had done for other saints as they served Him. I needed God Himself to mightily show up on my behalf. I was not asking for selfish reasons to exalt myself by calling down a miracle from heaven. It was the name of the Lord and His glory that was being challenged.

When I opened my eyes from praying, I looked to the left and saw a wall of water falling about three hundred yards away that was so heavy, it obscured anything from being seen on the other side of it. One of my teenagers saw it and quickly suggested we try to move the meeting into the small bus we had travelled in to the village. It was too small to accommodate the whole group and would probably have been the final disruption that would have ended the service.

"God's not going to let Satan stop this service," I told him. God had been moving in the hearts of the villagers as testimonies and Gospel messages were given. In my heart, I said, "Father, I trust you. I know that it looks like we're going to get drenched, but you stopped the sun and the moon for Joshua when he was fighting your battles. So stop the rain for us."

I looked up again after my prayer. This time, I looked to my right and saw the wall of water was coming down on the other side of the village. I looked to my left and saw the wall of water still coming down at the same spot I had last seen it. Wide eyed, I looked in front and behind me and saw it was raining hard all around us but we were dry in the middle of this circle of rain. I could hardly believe it.

At the end of the service, there were tears in most of the people's eyes. There were hugs and smiles given as the villagers returned home, thinking about what they had seen and heard. We boarded the bus and began the trip back to the missionary station at the bottom of the mountain. Silence hung in the air like an eagle riding the wind, seeing the world from a perspective those bound to the earth can never know. Awed by the power of God, I felt I had seen something too sacred for words. I just wanted to sit there and soak it all in.

Finally, after a long period of silence, our missionary friend broke the stillness. "Well, I hope you're happy," he said in a sarcastic tone. A puzzled look came over my face. He saw it and continued. "These people only get two or three good rains a year, and you prayed that one away." We burst out in laughter, and the bus buzzed with conversation the rest of the way home as each one shared what they saw and felt.

That Sunday, at the little mission church at the bottom of the mountain, twelve people showed up for the church service from that village. After church, they told the missionary the reason they had come was because of what they had seen our God do for us that day in their village. Three months after returning to the US, I received a letter from our missionary telling how the village had opened up to be evangelized. They had to run an old school bus up there to accommodate all the people who wanted to come to church each Sunday.

As I face the challenges of each new day, I often remember that miracle and am encouraged to believe God is waiting to do the same in any life that looks to Him for the miracle He knows they need. However, this kind of faith did not happen overnight for me. My journey of faith and understanding how it works in a person's daily life began even before I was a believer.

Though my dad died when I was two months old, my mother told me stories of his amazing faith. She said he would "pray through" on a matter and live in the light of what God had told him. One such story was about my dad being called by someone in the community to pray over their child who was sick and at the point of death.

This was during the time of the Great Depression. There were few doctors available in a rural community and even less money to pay them. Dad went to the home, but before he prayed for the child, he stood silently over the baby to seek God in the matter. After a time of silent meditation, he announced that the baby was sick due to a secret sin in the father's life. Furthermore, the baby would not recover until the man would get "right with God." The father immediately did so, and the baby's health was restored at that moment.

I didn't just have to hear about faith. I observed it on a daily basis in my mother's life. We or someone else would have some financial or material need, and she would just pray in what was needed. Honoring God with her possessions was a regular way of life. She believed if you honored God with your money, you would always have and always be able to give to help others.

An example of this was when my mother gave money to our neighbors when they were having a financial crisis. Both of them had good jobs but were still unable to have the money they needed to make their house payment and were in danger of losing their home. My mother gave them the money they needed. You need to understand that we lived on Social Security checks from my father's death benefit. In addition to that, she babysat kids for one dollar a day. The fee included lunch and a snack during the day. Needless to say, there was not a lot left over to add to the monthly Social Security check.

Even though I had every reason to exercise faith in God, I did not experience it at work in my own life until I was in the third grade. I wasn't a Christian yet but knew God was real. The day before at church, the preacher had preached a message on faith. These were the days before children's church, so I was in the adult service. He preached that we don't have because we don't ask, quoting James 4:2.

That Monday at school, I decided to put that statement to the test. It was after lunch and I was by myself sitting in a swing on the playground. You could get ice cream during that time if you had the money. Back then, ice cream cost a dime, but that didn't matter because my pockets were empty. As I sat in that swing, I prayed, "God, I sure would like to have some ice cream. Would you send me some money?"

I had no idea how He was going to do it. I just asked like He said I was supposedly to do. As I waited, I swung my feet back and forth over the rut in the ground made by years of usage by children. To my surprise and amazement, there in the rut was a quarter. It had been covered by the dust and left there by God for me to find. I not only bought one but two ice creams and had a nickel left over for later. Thus began my journey to live by faith.

As a young Christian, I only pulled faith out in emergencies. If I couldn't handle a situation or needed help to get what I wanted, I applied my faith to the task. God, most of the time, granted some form of the request which I had asked. He is gracious that way. However, I couldn't explain why it didn't work all the time. Maybe I had not earned it by doing some good deed or didn't understand how to use the right spiritual key that would unlock the door of miracles to get what I wanted.

One day during my devotions, I believe I had stumbled on the reason for my occasional failure to get that which I had asked. Matthew 17:20 says, "And Jesus said unto them, because of your unbelief: for truly I say unto you, if you have the faith as a grain of mustard seed, you shall say unto this mountain, move from here to another place and it shall move; and nothing shall be impossible unto you." That had to be it. I just wasn't believing enough. So I set out to believe.

The problem was, I couldn't have told you the difference between my believing and getting what I wanted and the believing that left me empty handed. At that time, I didn't stop to think about it that way. It had to be that God was testing me to believe more sincerely. I had to prove myself to God by believing the impossible. I determined to do just that.

There are a lot of stories I could write about in believing the impossible. The majority of them would actually end in a miracle being provided by God. However, there were those that would end with that for which I was believing not happening. I would step out on faith, making statements and actions that were the proof of my faith but ended up looking like an idiot for believing the impossible.

One such story happened while I was the music and youth pastor at a church in North Carolina. God was doing amazing things there. It had grown from a country church of about ninety to a church of over four hundred. We were seeking God for greater ways to reach people with the gospel and grow them in their faith. A couple in the church offered a piece of property to the church on which we could possibly build a youth camp.

In talking with them about the property, they told me of a local story that said a large treasure of gold had been hidden there at the end of the Civil War. The Confederate Army had collected it to fund a last-ditch effort to win the war. Through the years, some people had periodically looked for it. They suggested that if we cleared the property or did excavation work, someone from the church should be there, just in case.

The church didn't have the money for building a camp, but I was going to believe it by going up to the property and find the gold. I know that may seem foolish to you, but that is what believing the impossible is all about. It doesn't make sense until God does it. For over a year, I would go up to the fifteen acres of wooded mountainside and hunt for gold. I went in all types of weather: rain, snow, and extreme cold and heat. Each time, I convinced myself I was purifying my faith to the point that God would have to answer with a miracle.

After several attempts, I tried fasting and long times of prayer to aid in finding the gold. I asked God to show me where to dig. I dug holes all over the place. The ground was rock hard, but I had to be faithful on my end for God to be faithful on His. After a year, I gave up. Then six months later, while having my devotions in a passage that talked about faith, the idea came to my mind to go again. The weather was horrible. It was snowing and windy.

I argued with myself about how illogical it was to do this. However, the idea of this being the final test, with the gold just waiting for me to find it, tormented me. You guessed it. I went, prayed, and dug. After about an hour and having no feeling in my fingers, I headed back to the car, shovel in hand. I was mad. Mad at myself for being stupid enough to do it. Mad at God for not delivering the miracle for which I had believed.

"I can't trust You," I complained to God. "I had faith. I completely believed. How can I have confidence in You leading in my life if You haven't delivered the gold to me? How can I challenge others to trust You when you may or may not come through for them?" The Holy Spirit spoke these words so plainly to me, I can still hear them in my mind. "Did I ever tell you there was gold up there? Was I the one who told you to go dig?" The question floored me. "Well, no," I said. "It was my idea, but I was basing it on what You said about faith in the Bible."

"I never promised to bless your plans in faith but Mine, and I did. You did find gold," God informed me. My mind immediately went to several scriptures on faith. First Peter 1:7 says, "That the trial of your faith being much more precious than gold that perishes, though it be tried with fire, might be found unto praise and honour and glory at the appearing of Jesus Christ."

"Trust in the Lord with all your heart; and lean not unto your own understanding. In all your ways acknowledge him, and he shall direct your paths" (Proverbs 3:5–6).

The gold I found that day was a clearer understanding of how faith works. I had been operating under the assumption that faith in faith was the key to moving mountains. I would come up with the plans and believe God to make them happen. God taught me in that moment that my faith should be in His character and His perfect desire to give me what I need. It is not about what I want. I am to bring my requests to Him but not dictate how He meets them.

Faith works best when you realize God has a perfect plan based on your decisions and His ability to take them and weave them into something far superior to what you can do. Look to Him. Know His heart, His mind, His ways. Make choices that are in line with who the Scriptures say He is and what He does. If you do that, you will see the sovereign hand of God move in your life.

Application

We live at a time when many people are facing a crisis of faith. Whom do you believe and what do you believe in? If you are a young person, I advise you to pick an area of need or desire in your life and begin looking for a promise in the Bible that addresses the need. You can look up words that are associated with your need in the concordance at the back of most Bibles to find a promise. You can also ask someone who knows the Bible to suggest some verses for you to look at. Pray and ask God to show you what He is promising to do for you, and wait and see what happens.

For people who are middle-aged adults, I encourage you to take an honest look at what you have put your faith in up to this point. What has proven untrustworthy and what has proven dependable? You may have made your choices based on some accurate information but have put it together in a way that has brought you to wrong conclusions, causing you to put your faith in the wrong things. There is a difference between facts and truth. Let me give you an example of what I mean.

It is a fact that I regularly sleep with two females. Sometimes, it is not the same two females. This may lead you to believe I am a sex pervert. However, the truth is my daughter or one of my grand-daughters sometimes slip into the bed with my wife and I, and falls asleep. Trust how the Bible says things work best and begin doing it God's way. I have heard the definition of *insanity* is doing the same thing over and over but expecting different results.

To people like myself who are in the sunset years of their lives, it is hard to look back on most of your life and admit you have been wrong. Not doing it won't change the fact that you have been. "Better late than never" is an old but wise saying to apply to your situation. Put your faith in God and watch Him use your past choices, good and bad, as a life lesson by which others can profit. Your life is coming to an end. By faith, let it end heading in the right direction.

Pugh proverb: "There are no great Christians, only Christians who know the greatness of their God."

Scripture verses: Hebrews 13:20–21, Mark 12:30–31, Romans 7:14–25, Galatians 2:16–21

When I was young, probably no older than ten, I heard a sermon that used as an illustration something out of the life of one of the great preachers in history. I can't remember who it was, but I will never forget what was said. "The world has yet to see what God can do through a person who is totally surrendered to him," was the statement that was heard by this great preacher when he was just a boy. He pledged that "by the grace of God, I will be that man."

Those words burned in my soul. I believe in the heart of every born-again Christian is the desire to give God everything. At the end of the service, the invitational song was "I Surrender All," and I made a commitment to God just like that famous preacher did when he was a boy. I determined that "by the grace of God, I will be that man."

I would like to tell you, I became the epitome of what a "world's greatest Christian" should look like, but that would be a lie. I did, however, start my journey to perfection. You see, I was brought up in a home with high standards, both Christian standards and those applying to any endeavor in life. My mother made me act like a Christian long before I became one. Winning was expected in my family. Being the best was the norm. I had three older brothers that would settle for nothing less.

Verses like Hebrews 13:20–21 stuck in my brain. "Now the God of peace that brought again from the dead our Lord Jesus, that great shepherd of the sheep, through the blood of the everlasting covenant, equip you with everything good that you may do his will, working in you that which is well pleasing in his sight, through Jesus Christ; to whom be glory for ever and ever. Amen." The world's greatest Christian would have to be perfect to achieve the title.

I would "love the Lord my God with all my heart, and with all my soul, and with all my mind, and with all my strength…and love my neighbor as myself" (Mark 12:30–31). To accomplish this, I threw myself into every good work. As a junior-age boy, I would go into the jail and witness to prisoners. I brought my first convert to Christ by the age of thirteen. I was a leader in my youth group, involved in every activity and outreach. At public school, though popular, I was laughed at by teammates in locker rooms for not listening to their dirty jokes. Coaches and teachers would sometimes belittle me for my Christian standards.

However, the harder I worked at cleaning up the outside of my life, the more I became aware of inward evil. Pride, lust, fear, jealousy, and so on lived in the corners of my heart. Anger and self-hatred boiled inside me whenever I made even the slightest mistake. I couldn't show it though. After all, you can't achieve the world's-greatest-Christian title admitting to such struggles.

Therefore, I used it all to fuel my quest for perfection. At the age of eleven, I surrendered to go into full-time Christian ministry. God did genuinely call me, but subconsciously, it became another proof of my commitment to my goal. My last two years of high school, God opened the door for me to attend a wonderful Christian school. I was no longer persecuted for my Christian character but was applauded for it. I won the Christian Character Award in my senior year but was no better in my soul for the winning of it.

At the Bible college I attended, I continued to excel. In my first year, I traveled with a singing group representing the college that summer. By my second year, I was selected to be a resident assistant, in charge of my floor at the dorm. The last two years, I was head resident assistant, in charge of the whole men's dorm after the administration went home. Everyone looked to me for wisdom and advice, thinking I had the whole Christian life thing worked out. I knew better.

To give you an example of this, let me recount a story from my Bible college days. It was my junior year, and it was exam time. Because of working in a church as the youth minister, playing college sports, and the demands of being head resident assistant, I was under the gun to get ready for exams the next morning. I always took an overload of classes each semester and had four big exams staring me in the face. It was four in the morning when I heard a knock at the door. Some lovesick guy on my floor couldn't sleep because of the problems he was having with his girl and saw my light was on and wanted to talk.

The thought that came into my mind at that point both shocked and convicted me. The words, "Go to hell, I am busy," ran through my mind. I had just counseled him about his relationship several hours before. He was the reason I was up so late in the first place. To continue my quest to be the world's greatest Christian I reluctantly opened the door. While going back over the same advice I had given him earlier, the Holy Spirit worked on me. The hypocrisy of my heart while appearing so "holy" ate at me.

For days on end, I struggled with it. I even thought about getting up before the whole school at one of the chapels and telling everyone what a hypocrite I was, nothing but a miserable failure at living a victorious Christian life. However, God wouldn't let me. He showed me that I was trying to beat myself up until I felt I could let go of the guilt I was feeling. I cried out to Him like never before to show me how to be free from the monster of condemnation that tormented my soul.

He directed my attention to Romans 7:14–25. This was not a new passage to me. Many times in my devotions, I had studied the book of Romans and had thought about these scriptures. I knew that God's law was perfect and that I was failing in walking it out. I identified with the frustration I could sense in Paul's words. "For I do not understand my own actions. For I do not do what I want, but I do the very thing I hate." He even repeats that frustration again in verse 19. "For I do not do the good that I want, but the evil I do not want is what I keep doing."

However, in times past, I struggled with Paul saying, "Now then it's not me that's doing it, but sin that dwells in me." How could Paul not take responsibility for his own actions? He had a free will given to him by God. The devil could not make him sin, nor would God do it. He had to choose sin. Therefore, he was at fault. He was still somehow flawed and therefore a failure. I know I felt that way about myself.

This time, however, God broke through the wrong thinking that had clouded my understanding of scripture. To do that, He focused my attention on verse 18. "For I know that in me [that is, in my flesh] there is no good thing: for my will wants to do right, but how to carry it out in my actions I can't make happen." The Holy Spirit said to my heart, "The desire, which indicates your character, who you really are, is perfect. You have been made that way through salvation. The problem is how to get the perfection out in your actions and attitude."

My mistake was in trying to improve my flesh. I believed that through my saved willpower, I could make my flesh obey God. This was in direct contradiction to "in my flesh dwells no good thing." God showed me that I had been "saved by grace and not by works, so that no one can boast" (Ephesians 2:8–9). My attempts to obey God by my saved willpower came from a thinking that was programed in my mind before Christ came into my life. I was trying to prove my perfection by improving my flesh, which at its root is pride. I needed to walk as a Christian the same way I came to Christ—by faith, not by self-effort.

To further show me this truth, God took me to Galatians 2:16–21. This passage starts with the principle "that a man is not justified by the works of the law, but by the faith of Jesus Christ." Obviously, the law is good, but doing it can never justify me. It can only show me my failure to fulfill it and my need of Christ's righteousness. The passage goes on to state that if I adopt the thinking I had as an unsaved individual to guide me as a Christian, I would make myself believe that I was still a transgressor and not the perfect righteousness of Jesus Christ. Feelings of failure and defeat would dominate my thinking.

God brought me to understand that the soul or spirit of rebellion and imperfection that was born in my body was nailed to the cross with Christ. He had paid for its evil and had given me His perfection to become my new soul or spirit. That is what is meant by a Christian having the *imputed* righteousness of Christ. I had been frustrating the grace of God from guiding my thoughts, actions, and attitudes by trying to fulfill the requirements of the law by my saved willpower. To seal this idea in my mind, God gave me two illustrations that I use to this day to keep these truths at the center of my heart.

The first illustrates what it means to have "imputed righteousness" (Romans 4:6). Imagine that you are a penniless pauper living under a bridge. All you own are the ragged clothes on your back. One day, a limo pulls up and a well-dressed man gets out. He introduces himself as a gazillionaire who wants to give to you a gazillion dollars if you will give him permission to do so by signing the deposit slip he has with him. You ask him, "What's the catch?" He assures you he wants to do so just because he cares about you. It's free for the receiving.

You don't understand it all but think, *What have I got to lose?* So you sign the deposit slip hoping the impossible is true. He gives you a temporary checkbook and instructs you that if you want something, all you have to do is write a check for it. He further explains that as soon as he gets back in the limo and pulls away, he will make the deposit electronically and you will be a gazillionaire.

The limo pulls away and you numbly walk back toward the bridge under which you currently live. You are trying to process it all when another guy who lives under the bridge comes up to you and asks, "What was that all about?" You tell him the story that explains how you are now a gazillionaire. He just bursts into uproarious laughter. "Would a gazillionaire live under a bridge? Do gazillionaires dress the way you are dressed? Do they eat out of a garbage can? You are a fool to believe what that man said."

You have to admit, the answer to all his questions is no. A sinking feeling begins to grip your heart. However, the checkbook in your hand is real, and you decide to give it a try. You go to the McDonalds where you usually rummage through the garbage cans for food and go in. The young lady at the counter gives you a mean look and asks, "What do you want?" You nervously ask for a cheeseburger and a glass of water. "How are you going to pay for it?" she demands. You show her the checkbook. "Did you steal that?"

"No, a man gave it to me," you reply.

She reluctantly places the order and gives you the price of the meal. You write out the check for $1.05 just hoping it all works out. The cashier runs the check through their monitor to see if the funds are available for the purchase. All zeros come up on the display, which makes you think you are still a penniless pauper, but there is a light flashing on the machine with a code. She calls for her manager to interpret the code, and they find that the display is not large enough to register the complete amount available. There is a one in front of all those zeroes.

The manager calls the bank and after a hard-to-believe conversation with the bank, tells the cashier to give you whatever you want. Stunned, you sit down and enjoy for the first time a fresh cheeseburger and a cold glass of water. For the next several days, you repeat the process and come to expect to get your food. Emboldened by your success, you decide to order the top-of-the-line meal on the menu. It worked, and you noticed you are being treated with more respect. You decided to test out the checkbook on other items: clothes, shoes, renting an apartment, everything. Each time, it worked. Soon, you are living a good life equal to everyone else but not at the level of a gazillionaire. You are happy and comfortable in your middle-class lifestyle.

One day, the man who had given you the money drives up to you and asks what you have been doing with the money he had given you. When you tell him, you can see a troubled look on his face. You become nervous, afraid he is going to ask for the money back. After all, you had not earned a penny of it. It all came from him. Seeing the fear in your face, he says, "The money I gave you is yours just as much as if you earned every penny of it. Legally, I could not get it back even if I wanted to do so. However, you could be enjoying so much more if you understood how rich I have made you. It's up to you. You could go back and live under the bridge where I found you and eat out of the garbage cans if you want, but that would not change the fact that you are a gazillionaire. The level you live at is up to you. I encourage you to live fully."

Righteousness is mine as if I had earned perfection, even though it was given to me—imputed—in salvation by Jesus Christ. His work has made me His righteousness. I have the same desire to obey God that Jesus had when He walked the face of the earth. The only difference is I live in a body that fights me on letting it out. If I want to live as if this is not true, I live in the truths seen in Galatians 2:16–21. I try by my own saved willpower to prove I am righteous rather than living in the power of the cross. I frustrate the grace of God.

The next illustration that helped me see I am the perfect righteousness of Christ is one the Holy Spirit gave me one day when I was having my devotions but was really discouraged about my recent behavior. I was moaning about my discouragement when the Lord reminded me of a commercial I had seen that day. It was the Staples commercial where all you have to do is push the red Staples button that says "Easy," and it would be. God said, "If I had a magic red button that if you pushed, you would give away your free will but you would never again disobey or fail me, would you push it?"

"In the blink of an eye, I would," was my response.

"Then, as I told you in Romans chapter 7, your inner man is perfect. The problem is your power source to get it out. Focus on me and what I have done for you. Let thanksgiving and praise be your focus and not proving anything about you."

Since then, I have gone deeper by the Holy Spirit's help into these truths and have boiled them down to the Pugh proverb: "There are no great Christians, only Christians who know the greatness of their God." May you, by faith in Jesus Christ and what He has accomplished for you, walk in the light of this truth.

Application

There are two things I would suggest to help anyone apply this proverb to their life. The first is to make a list of all the positive things about yourself and what you have done. Take your time, even if it takes a few days. Then, as an act of worship, symbolically give them back to the One Who gave them to you by burning the list.

Secondly, I would start a list of every good thing you know about God. You can keep it in a Bible, put it on your refrigerator, or in your room on a mirror, anywhere you can be reminded to think about it. Add to the list things for which you are thankful to God for doing or giving you. You will find these two simple suggestions will bring you closer to God.

Pugh proverb: "Satan does not care who is right or wrong, only who is under his influence."

Scripture verses: Ephesians 6:11–12; Romans 6:12–13, 16

I love to debate. Debate is not the same as arguing. Arguing, in my mind, means you must win the verbal exchange at all costs. You cannot concede any point of logic or fact. That would indicate your opponent is winning in the battle and you are losing ground. I had been brought up in a strong Christian home that taught dishonesty is sin, even intellectual dishonesty. Therefore, I gravitated toward debate. That is not to say I have not fallen into the sin of arguing, but I can't feel I have won if I have to cheat.

Debate is the verbal or written ability to present facts, information, and illustrations that would lead a person to the same conclusion I have come to and am currently presenting to them. Debate, I had told myself, was for the betterment of people of lesser intellectual capabilities, confused souls that needed my guidance to improve their life and way of thinking. They needed to be straightened out. I had also observed in my young life that people who could debate well usually got what they wanted. They were the leaders, the movers and shakers of this world. So I decided to uses my mental and verbal talents to this noble end.

I became good at it. It made me feel powerful. After all, who wants to be wrong? Little did I realize there was an underlying layer of pride that was fed by the fact of being right all the time. A monster was growing inside me that needed to be killed. I couldn't see it, but others had noticed it. However, they were unwilling or too afraid to mention it to me. Ironically, maybe they felt like they couldn't win the argument to show it to me. Thank God for the people He puts in your life. I have a best friend who shall remain nameless. You know who you are. He was willing to challenge me on the blind spot of debating. One day, we were driving from a gymnasium and were talking about some subject from different points of view. I will never forget the words he said to me after several minutes of debate. "You are the most opinionated person I have ever known. I don't mean that in a bad way. You just never believe you are wrong."

"If I thought I was wrong, I would change," was my response.

That conversation, however, sparked a mental debate in my own mind. For the first time, I wondered if I came across as a know-it-all. As stated in the previous proverb, I wanted to be the perfect Christian. If I was a know-it-all, then I was in sin and failing in my quest to be perfect. Debating with yourself can be quite exhausting. I gave up on trying to win the debate with myself. I am pretty good at it after all and decided to declare it a draw.

God had other ideas. It seems He had allowed me to develop an attraction to women with strong personalities. When you are dating someone like that, debate is a given. Most of the time, I allowed the girl I was dating to have her way. That was the loving thing to do, but I still debated the issues in my mind. I was able to let go of being right because I had time away from them to acknowledge my "right-ness" without them seeing it.

However, when you are married, that is a different story. You eat at the same table, sleep in the same bed, and go to the same bathroom. It is hard to get away to have that private I'm-right moment. Plus, by that time, you know each other well enough to read on the face and body language that which is unspoken. My wife could tell I thought she was wrong and I was right, which I was. The debate would continue with me mounting more and more evidence that should cause her to see things my way, the right way.

It hardly ever did. It only seemed to make her mad, and I didn't want that. However, I couldn't lie and say she was right if I didn't believe it to be so. How could I help her see the light and get out of this mess? For years, I didn't have a good answer to the question. Satan knew that and used it to his advantage to try and rob my wife and me of the joys God had intended for our marriage.

We seemed to be on a regular basis at odds with each other on what was the best way to fold a shirt, load the dishwasher, how to spend money, and so on. If my wife and I had not been strong in our faith and belief that God had made us for each other and were willing to forgive or overlook things in love, we would have grown apart. That didn't change the fact we had to find God's answer to this dilemma.

God answers prayers in the most unusual way sometimes. I don't remember what the issue was about, but we were at it again. I was so clearly in the right. I couldn't understand how she couldn't see it. She was putting up her strawman arguments, and I was knocking them down with brilliant, undeniable logic. She knew she was wrong but was mad and tried to use upping the volume in her voice to cause me to back down. Satan got ahold on me, and I decided to return what she was giving. "I'll give her a taste of her own medicine," was the satanically placed idea in my head. I began to yell at her and in doing so knew I was out of control.

I walked out of the house in need of God's intervention to deliver me from my runaway thoughts and emotions. The Holy Spirit brought to mind the scripture in Ephesians 6:12. "For we wrestle not against flesh and blood, but against principalities, against powers, against the rulers of the darkness of this world, against spiritual wickedness in high places." I realized I was being manipulated by Satan to do his bidding. He was using me and my approach in the situation to tempt my wife to feel I was putting her down and that the conversation was about who the winner was and who the loser was.

He then reminded me of Romans 6:12, 13, 16, which states, "Let not sin therefore reign in your mortal body, that you should obey it in its lustful desires. Neither yield your physical body as instruments of unrighteousness to commit sin: but yield yourselves unto God, as those that are alive from the dead, and your physical body as instruments of righteousness unto God. Don't you know that to whom you yield yourselves servants to obey, his servants you are to whom you obey; whether of sin unto death, or of obedience unto righteousness."

I became convicted of the sin of pride. Satan had so focused my attention on being right I could not see how I was playing right into his hands. I wasn't being empowered by God to help my wife. I was being used by Satan to cause my wife to sin. You can never win a debate with the Holy Spirit, and I didn't even try. I humbled myself and confessed my sin to God. I truly repented.

That changed everything. After repenting, I asked God to help me do His will in discussing the current issue with my wife. I started by asking her forgiveness and then suggested we pray together about the issue before revisiting the problem. It was as if the sun had come out after a winter's snow. The problem seemed to just melt away as we sought God's will, even if we did start from two different points of view. After that, my focus in any debate was, *Am I under the control of the Holy Spirit or am I being spiritually hijacked by the devil?*

It is a good thing God taught me this lesson. As someone in the ministry, I have avoided Satan's traps on many occasions by remembering this proverb. One such occasion happened in the church I am currently pastoring. We were adding on to our existing building and were putting in some new swinging doors that opened into the sanctuary. The men that installed them suggested they be left a natural color. A leading woman in our church thought they should be stained early American and began to lobby for that idea. This spurred the men to dig in their heels and fight for the natural look they liked.

In a few weeks, the church had become so polarized on the issue it was hard to worship or preach because of the struggle. From the pulpit, I addressed the problem. "No more souls are going to be won to Christ whether the doors are stained natural or early American. God doesn't care about the color, but He has let this controversy happen to show us our hearts before God. Satan is using this to divide us that he might get a foothold in this church." I then stated the Pugh proverb, "Satan does not care who is right or wrong, only who is under his influence." God used that truth to break Satan's hold on the situation and bring repentance and unity back to the church. We left the door a neutral color, but more importantly, our souls rejoiced for the lesson learned.

Over the years, I have applied this truth to numerous situations dealing with people. As others have learned and applied it, they have given testimony to its power. The next time you are in a "debate," don't forget to ask yourself the question: Am I under the control of the Holy Spirit or the control of Satan? Do I care more about being Christ-like or being "right"?

Application

The next time you find yourself in a heated exchange with someone, imagine a person holding a gun to their head. The person with the gun is making them do and say to you the things that are upsetting you. Would you hold the person being held hostage responsible for upsetting you? Would you shoot the person with the gun by putting a bullet through the body of the person held hostage? I would hope not. To defeat Satan's grip on you and the other person, you must speak the truth in love. Forgive and set both of you free.

Pugh proverb: "People are the pits, including me; the only one you can trust is God."

Scripture verses: Romans 3:10, 12; Proverbs 29:25; Hebrews 13:5, 8

You may think upon reading this proverb that it came out of the life of someone who has been mistreated or was done wrong all their life. Betrayal usually makes a person mistrust. However, my thinking in this matter has not been jaded by such an upbringing. My mom never locked the doors of our house until she was eighty-three and then only at night. Our house was always open to anyone as a welcoming place to come.

As an eight-year-old boy, during the summer, I walked a mile and a half to and from Little League practice twice a week. It was not uncommon for someone to stop and offer me a ride. Usually, I knew the person who offered the ride. Most peoples' faces were familiar in our small rural community. However, sometimes I did not. People had always been kind to me on many levels during my childhood, so that is not the basis for my proverb.

Growing up in our country church made it easy for me to know a person based not only on what they sang and said on Sunday but how they lived the rest of the week. Most of the adults, I had known all my life. At one time or another, they had taught me in Sunday school, sang with me in the choir, led vacation Bible school, or gave a testimony in church. They were good people, as people go, but not without flaws.

I remember as a junior-age boy a church business meeting that had gotten out of control. People I looked up to were behaving as if Christian character was not important but getting your way was. I was saddened by that but not disillusioned. I had been taught from the Bible that man was born with a sinful nature, and even after salvation, that mindset could still rear its ugly head. Romans 3:10 states, "As it is written, there is none righteous, no, not one, for all have sinned and come short of the glory of God."

So-called reality TV is a good representation of this truth. People make "friendships," pledging to be there for each other and watch each other's backs. However, they are only using one another, working some angle that will benefit them. When the time is right, a knife will be plunged into the back they are supposedly guarding. They may like you, but not as much as they like themselves. I have never known anyone to vote themselves off the island to allow their "friend" to stay. This life philosophy is true for the majority of people with which I come in contact.

There are, however, those rare individuals that truly do not want to let you down. People who love you and desire the best for you can still not be there for you when you need them for one reason or another. My dad died when I was two months old. I am sure he loved me but was not there for me when I needed a dad growing up. Mom died several years ago at the age of ninety-three. I miss her greatly. Family and friends grow up and move away, living their own lives. Time and space make them absent from you when you really want them there with you to lean on.

That is why most people go looking for a mate they can live with till death do they part. People seek someone to build their life around, thinking that will bring stability and safety both physically and emotionally, but it won't. I tried that in my own dating life. Three times, I fell in love. And three times, I watched as they broke up with me. Thank God, one came back.

Even though I have a great marriage, there are times my lovely wife is not there for me. Satan has hijacked her and used her to come at me. People say a successful marriage is fifty-fifty. If that is true, then half the time, you are missing something you need or want from them. I have found that to be successful at marriage, you have to be willing to go one hundred over zero, if necessary. Sometimes, even the best of people give you nothing. Romans 3:12 puts it this way. "They are all gone out of the way, they are together become unprofitable: there is none that doeth good, no, not one."

Because of the failure of friends and loved ones to be the perfect support on which to depend, people determine to only depend on themselves. Boy, have I found that to be a great mistake. The person that has disappointed me the most, the one who has every reason to be there for me but time after time betrays me, is me. I have dishonored what I believe in many times. I have done things that have brought shame and disgrace into my life. There were times in my life I wished I were someone else so I could beat the tar out of me for what I have done.

That is why I embrace what Proverbs 29:25 says. "The fear of man [putting your trust and dependence in a person] bringeth a snare, but whoever puts his trust in the Lord shall be safe." God has never let me down. That is not just preacher talk. I have deserved God walking away from me, but He hasn't nor will He ever. Hebrews 13:8 states, "Jesus Christ, the same yesterday, today and forever."

People will often ask me, "If you don't trust people, then how are you so open to everyone?"

"It's because I don't depend on them as the source for what I want and need. They can't fail me if I don't depend on them. I expect people to fail me. I fail myself. However, God never has failed me and never will." Hebrews 13:5 says, "Keep your life free from the love of money, and be content with such things as you have; for God will never leave you, nor forsake you." That's why, God is the only one we can trust.

Application

There are two steps in a process that will allow you to apply this proverb in your life. Forgiveness is at the heart of step one and step two. Make a list of all the people whom you put your trust in that have let you down. Next, make a list of the people you have let down. Privately, read them out loud one by one. After each entry, say out loud, "You are forgiven." At the end of reading them all, tear the paper into little pieces and burn them.

The second step is a prayer of commitment to look to God and not people for what you need in life. Here is a sample prayer. "Dear God, I have sinned by looking to myself or others to do for me what only You can do. Forgive me. I want to trust You but struggle to do so. Help me, In Jesus name, amen."

Pugh proverb: "Satan is the enemy; people are the prize to be won."

Scripture verses: Ephesians 6:11–13, Matthew 7:1–5, Luke 15:4–7, John 3:16–17

As stated in the last Pugh proverb, people are the pits. The recent presidential debates are a good example of this. An honest debate on the issues was not what we watched but two political leaders acting like children. The majority of the worlds' problems stem from not handling people correctly. Nations are at war, each seeing the other as the enemy. Even within countries, there are ethnic, social, political, and ideological groups that struggle with each other to gain control of their culture. Religion should be the oil that, through love and understanding, makes things run without friction in a society, but it seems to be the greatest offender.

Unfortunately, the home also has become a major battleground in recent days for conflict. Sure, there always have been challenges in our homes, but most families found a way to work through their differences. Today, the divorce rate predicts half of marriages will not last. Of those that do, around 80 percent experience marital unfaithfulness during their years together. Fractured homes produce wounded teens and children that take their anger and frustration to school with them, thus producing behavioral problems at school.

That was where my understanding of this proverb began to take shape. It was in my ninth-grade PE class. Our teacher was also the basketball coach, so he decided we were going to play basketball.

He chose the teams for us, pitting me against one of his star players. This guy looked like a young John Travolta or Fonzie from the old *Happy Days* show. He had a cockiness to him that was hard to ignore. I think the coach did it because he didn't like me because I was a Christian, and he wanted to make Christians look like weak pansies.

As we started to play, all I can say is God allowed an anointing of basketball skill to come upon me, and I was unstoppable. Midway through the game, my team was ahead by twenty points. Tim Beale, the John Travolta look-alike, was beyond frustrated. He took it personally that I was playing superior to him and wanted to stop me at all cost. He had no success at doing it.

Then, to my surprise, the teacher switched me to the other team and put Tim on the winning team I had been on. I guess he didn't want his star player to get schooled by someone who was not on his team. There were only about fifteen minutes left in the class. But during that time, God allowed me to bring the losing team back to win the game on a last-second shot made by, you guessed it, me.

Tim was furious, and my teacher just walked out of the gym shaking his head. Tim wanted to fight me. He started yelling how I had made him look bad and thought that I was better than him. Just then, three guys from our class stepped in from of me and said, "You'll have to get through us first." After a moment like what you may see in a gunfight scene in the old western movies, Tim backed down and went into the locker room.

I was grieved. I didn't want Tim to have a grudge against me. I wanted to reach Tim for Christ. John 3:16–17 had taught me God loved the world even though we didn't deserve it, and He wanted to save the world from eternal judgment. To do that, God came into our world as Jesus to show us He understands our pain and our needs. He wants a best-friend relationship with each of us. For me to reach Tim, I would have to enter his world and build a relationship with him.

Tim had always been a cocky jerk toward me. I didn't know why. The Holy Spirit prompted me to find out the reason. First, I started by going to him and apologizing for anything I had ever done to make it appear I was against him. I followed it up by complimenting him on his ability as displayed on the basketball court when the school team played. Lastly, I offered to buy him a candy bar at the snack shop as a kind of peace offering. He took me up on the offer, and we agreed to put the past behind us.

In the coming days, I made every effort to be Tim's friend. I prayed for Him, asking God to give me ways to make him my friend. As Tim began to trust me, he started to open up and share his life story. It was one of hardship. His parents had divorced when he was young, and he had not seen his father in years. His mother worked all the time, just trying to make ends meet. He and his little sister were alone most of the time. Tim was literally raising her. It put a lot of pressure on him. They lived in an old trailer that made him feel like he was second-rate.

Satan had so crushed the life out of him that he was acting out his pain by mistreating others. He was like a wounded animal, snapping and snarling at anyone who came close to the wounded areas in his life. His mind was clouded by the devil in order for Satan to keep Tim in his grip. I had the medicine named Jesus Christ that could heal his broken heart, if only I could get past his snapping and snarling to administer it.

Tim, in time, admitted he was jealous of me. I had something he wanted but didn't know how to get it for himself without stealing it from me by putting me down. That was my opening to share with him the good news of God's love for him. Tim accepted Christ as his Savior that day. He wanted to start coming to church, so we picked him up every week on the church bus. Tim came faithfully and grew as a result of soaking up God's unconditional love for him. He was transformed from a jerk to a wonderful brother in Christ.

God's heart is for every wandering or lost soul. Luke 15:4–7 is a parable Jesus used to demonstrate this fact. It says

> What man of you, having an hundred sheep, if he lose one of them, does not leave the ninety and nine in the wilderness, and go after the one which is lost, until he finds it? And when he has found it, he lays it on his shoulders, rejoicing.

> And when he comes home, he calls together his
> friends and neighbors, saying unto them, Rejoice
> with me for I have found my sheep which was
> lost. I say unto you, that likewise joy shall be in
> heaven over one sinner that repents, more than
> ninety and nine just persons, which need no
> repentance.

In the years to come, God sent me out as His representative to look for wandering and lost sheep on a regular basis. He was constantly putting lost causes and people with lots of spiritual baggage in my path. That's the problem with sheep. They get themselves in all sorts of trouble. To rescue them, you have to pay a price of aggravation, pain, and inconvenience. Many times, I would want to give up on a person, but the Holy Spirit wouldn't let me. He would say, "I need someone to love them for Me, and very few Christians are willing to love someone like them."

What I came to find out in time was the person who was the prize to be won was me. You see, a person can't remain the same and be used by God to help problem people. You must let God do a work of changing your spiritual eyesight to see people as Jesus sees them. Matthew 7:1–5 explains it this way.

> Judge not, that ye be not judged. For with what
> judgment ye judge, ye shall be judged: and with
> what measure ye mete, it shall be measured to you
> again. And why beholdest thou the mote that is
> in thy brothers' eye, but considerest not the beam
> that is in thine own eye? Or how wilt thou say
> to thy brother, Let me pull out the mote out of
> thine eye; and, behold, a beam is in thine own
> eye? Thou hypocrite, first cast out the beam out
> of thine own eye; and then shalt thou see clearly
> to cast out the mote out of thy brothers' eye.

There was a guy on my floor at Bible college that was a missionary kid. That means he grew up in a foreign country and not in "normal" American society. He was socially awkward. Some would even say he was weird. He tried way too hard to get people to like him. Because he didn't fit in very well, he picked up a nickname that underscored his ineptness. I was the resident assistant on the floor and interacted with him only as needed. For some reason—God teaching me a lesson—he attached himself to me. I could handle being around him for a maximum of about a half an hour. After that, I would find some excuse to get away from him so I could maintain my sanity.

I was complaining to God about him one day, asking why He put him in my path. "You need him," God said. "You are judgmental, self-centered, and unloving. What if I had let you be brought up in the circumstances he has faced? Remember, I told you to do unto others as you would have them do unto you." God had me. I was guilty as charged. In learning to really care about this individual and become his friend, I was rescued from sinful mindsets that would have limited what God could do in and through my life. Satan was the thorn in my flesh, not this person.

Satan has many times petitioned God to let him put some person in my path to trip me up in my Christian walk. As with Job, God has allowed the devil to come at me through people who I thought were my friends, or at least not my enemies. God's purpose is the same as it was with Job—to use me to help rescue people by pointing them to God's truth, and to enrich my life. When we stop seeing people as someone to be against and start seeing Satan as the real enemy, we will be cooperating with God in the situation. His power, wisdom, and protection is then at our disposal.

Several times in my coaching career, I have seen this to be true. One season as the varsity boys' coach, I had some players that thought they knew more about soccer than I did. They opposed me in big and small ways all season. I knew Satan was trying to ruin my testimony before my team and any fans that were aware of the conflict. I prayed hard for the Lord's grace, strength, and wisdom to guide me.

As we entered the postseason tournament, we had won only half of our games. I found out that text messages were being sent saying I was the problem. God directed me to call a team meeting and address the issue. I pointed out that the defiance to what I had instructed them to do was the problem. They had a rebellious spirit that Satan was using to rob them of playing up to their potential. During the tournament, God honored me and those who bought into the truths I had shared with them that day, and we won the tournament.

I am currently the varsity girls' soccer coach at the local high school. Last season, I found myself in a similar situation, this time with parents questioning my ability to coach. Before I go on, let me state that my credentials as a knowledgeable soccer coach are many. These few parents tried to get me fired. The girls' program had never won a postseason tournament game in the history of the program. Even though I had to bring up JV players to have enough to play our first-round game, God blessed and we won that game. I felt God had honored my desire to reach these people and my players for Christ. He had vindicated my leadership and decision-making skills in the eyes of my players and their parents.

Too many times, we lose sight of God's hand in situations. He came to set the captive free. We are His hands and His feet to do His work. If we won't love the jerk, be a friend to an obnoxious person, or seek to free people from the evil that enslaves them, then Satan continues to win. Let's fight the real enemy and not shoot his hostages.

Application

Choose someone in your life you don't particularly like and start praying for them. Ask God to show you why they act the way they do. Find out as much about the background of the person as you can, especially their formative years. Put yourself in their place and imagine how those life events would have affected you. Make a plan to do something nice for them. Continue the process until either they begin to change for the better or you do.

6

Pugh proverb: "If God doesn't do it, God doesn't want it."

Scripture verses: Genesis 4:3–7, 16:1–5; Exodus 1:11–15; Joshua 9; 1 Corinthians 3:11–15

The Bible is full of examples of people who did not understand or live by the biblical principles that birthed this proverb. Not only is the Bible full of them, but I have seen in life people making the same mistakes as these Bible characters. I am one of those people and will be using examples from my own life concerning this proverb that parallels theirs.

The first biblical character is Cain. In Genesis 4:3–7, we find the story of two different offerings being brought to God as an act of reverence. Cain brought an amazing array of vegetables he had grown of which any grocer would have been proud. Abel brought a lamb that was without spot or blemish. The Bible says that God had respect and accepted Abel's offering but rejected Cain's. This made Cain so mad he could not see straight. How could God not be impressed with such prize-winning vegetables as he had produced? In time, the thought of his best efforts being rejected by God made him depressed.

"And the Lord said unto Cain, Why are you angry, and why has your face fallen? If thou do well, will you not be accepted? And if you do not well, sin is crouching at the door." What God was saying to him was that Cain had grown those vegetables out of pride and presented them to God as evidence that God should be impressed with him. Cain was trying to earn God's love through what he could do for God. God's acceptance does not work that way.

That was what Abel understood. He brought an offering that was perfect because that was the way God had created the lamb—perfect. Abel could not take credit for that. Abel was following God's example as the pattern for acceptance He instituted when He sacrificed a lamb to cover Adam and Eve's sin. Only the work of God was sufficient to take away sin and produce righteousness. If God doesn't do it, God doesn't want it.

I had to come to this realization to be saved. Like Cain, I had spent most of my time in church trying to impress God with the good I could produce and present it to Him. He should want to save me because I was quite a catch. I could really help Him and be used to advance His kingdom. This is illustrated even in the circumstances surrounding the night of my conversion.

We were having a summer revival at my church. The youth choir was the featured music during the service, and I was the leading voice in the choir. I could really belt it out, even as an eight-year-old boy. Because of the volume and quality of my singing, I was placed in the center of the front row of the choir loft. We had just finished our last song and were asked to come down from the preaching platform.

Because the church was packed, I had to sit near the front where the old men usually sat. The preacher preached a simple yet powerful message that I could have given. It brought me under deep conviction. It seemed as if every time he pointed to the crowd, his finger touched my nose. He proclaimed that we are saved by grace and not by our works. Our good works were as filthy rags in God's sight. We could only be saved if we trusted in what Christ had done on the cross. God was looking for the blood of Jesus Christ applied to our heart as the reason His judgment would pass over us, not our self-efforts.

At the invitation, God was deeply convicting me of my need of Him. His conviction was so heavy, I couldn't continue singing the classic invitational hymn "Just As I Am." I just stood there, gripping the back of the pew in front of me, thinking, *I am too good to go forward. What would people think of me? They already think I am saved.*

Thank God there are a lot of verses to "Just As I Am." On the last verse, I finally couldn't take it any longer. I walked down the aisle, knelt at that altar, and surrendered my sinful soul to Christ. I repented of my pride and self-effort, and placed my faith in Jesus alone for my salvation. That night I knew, if God doesn't do it, God doesn't want it.

Even after you trust Christ as Savior, you can still violate this proverb as demonstrated by Abraham and Sarah in Genesis 16:1– 5. God had promised Abraham and Sarah they would have a child through which God would make a great nation that would bless the whole earth. Year after year, they waited for the promise to come true, and year after year, it did not happen. Sarah was past the child-bearing years, they thought, and Abraham was a hundred years old. Before it was too late, they decided to help God out.

In that culture, a slave was counted as the possession of the owner. Sarah wanted Abraham to have sex with her slave girl to produce a child that would be Sarah's by the law of that time. Abraham gave in to Sarah pressuring him, and a child was produced. However, God rejected the child, Ishmael, as the seed through which the promise would be fulfilled. Through a miracle years later, God gave Abraham and Sarah a son, Isaac, to be the child that would be used of God to fulfill His promise to Abraham. However, throughout history, there has always been conflict between the descendants of Isaac and Ishmael brought about by Abraham and Sarah's attempt to help God.

I have, on occasion, tried to help God out when He seemed too slow or unable to perform what I thought was needed. One such occasion concerned a guy in our church when I was a teenager. He was not a Christian, though his parents made him come to church regularly. I knew what he was like at school and knew he needed Jesus badly. So I began to make it my quest to get him saved. After months of praying for him and witnessing to him, he still wanted nothing to do with God.

That summer, at a youth revival his parents made him attend, the guy was hearing a great salvation message the speaker was giving. I just knew this had to be his moment to trust Christ as his Savior.

As the invitation was given and the music began, I looked for him to go forward, but he seemed unmoved. That's when it happened. I decided to help God out by playing Holy Spirit. I went to him and begged him to go forward. I even said I would go down with him. For several minutes, I pressured him to get saved. He finally went down to the altar as I triumphantly went with him. The minister had him come to the microphone afterward and asked him what he had done. He announced that he had gotten saved. Everyone was elated.

What I overheard the next day at school soon deflated that excitement. A friend of his had heard about his "salvation" and was asking him about it. The guy told his friend he only went forward to get people "off his back" and that he was embarrassed by the whole situation. He further told his friend he was going to tell his parents he was through going to church. After the blowup upon telling his parents the news, he moved out of their house and went to live with an uncle. I felt the guilt of being partially responsible for the whole situation. I learned that if God doesn't do it, God doesn't want it.

Moses tried to help God out in his early days of following Jehovah. You'll find the story in Exodus 2:11–15. Moses went down to where the Israelite slaves were making bricks for the pharaoh and saw an Egyptian taskmaster beating an Israelite slave. Moses had been created by God to deliver the slaves, but Moses was about to jump the gun and try to do it in the power of his flesh. Looking this way and that, he killed the Egyptian and buried him in the sand.

The next day while trying to settle an argument between two slaves, he finds out the murder is public knowledge. Moses realizes his days as a prince in the house of Pharaoh are over and runs for his life. For the next forty years, he runs from God's purpose for his life, feeling he is a failure. That's what comes from trying to do something for God instead of letting God do it through you.

Once again, I have done the same thing. I was teaching in the Christian school which the church I was working at had. The class was for juniors and seniors, and it was called church ministry. I wanted to do a fun, practical, big class project for the final grade in the class. I chose to do a paintball fun house.

You see, I had for thirteen years successfully designed and ran scary fun houses as an alternative to celebrating Halloween. They were famous all over the state of North Carolina, even drawing people from as far away as Georgia to come back every year to attend. As many as two thousand people a night, for three nights, would stand in line waiting to get in. At the end, we would present the gospel of Jesus Christ in various ways to those who had come. Every year, we had people make professions of faith through this ministry.

Because of this success, I felt I didn't need to pray about the paintball fun house as the final project. It made sense to me, and I just assumed God would bless it. After all, I was trying to train young people in how to minister for God in fun and unique ways. God had to bless my idea.

That was not the case. We worked for over a month getting the house and special effects ready. All was going well until the nights of the event. It rained hard for the three days we had planned to do the fun house. No one wanted to stand in line outside in that kind of weather just to shoot some paintball at popup targets and real people. Only 327 people came in three days. It was a miserable three nights for everyone.

When I complained to God about His lack of divine help in the situation, He asked me an interesting question. "Did I ever tell you to do this? This was your idea, not Mine. I let you go on with it so you could see what you could do without Me. Remember what happened to Joshua and the children of Israel in Joshua chapter 9? They assumed something based on their ability to assess the situation and entered into a treaty that caused problems throughout the history of Israel. I only bless what I do and command." If God doesn't do it, God doesn't want it.

First Corinthians 3:11–15 gives us a clear understanding of how God will deal with our efforts while here on earth. "For no one can lay a foundation other than that which is laid, which is Jesus Christ. Now if anyone builds upon this foundation with gold, silver, precious stones, wood, hay, straw; each one's work will become manifest, for the Day shall disclose it, by fire; and the fire shall test every man's work of what sort it is. If any man's work survive testing which he has done, he shall receive a reward. If any man's work shall be burned up, he shall suffer loss: but he himself shall be saved; but only as through fire." If God doesn't do it, God doesn't want it.

Application

You will need a bag of cookies for this application. Place all the cookies in a row on a table. You may have to make more than one row. One by one, imagine each cookie represents something good you believe you have done. At each cookie, ask yourself this question: "Did I do this so people would be impressed with me, or did I do it to point people to God?" If the answer is to impress people around you, throw the cookie into the trash can. After you go through all the cookies, eat the ones you didn't have to throw into the trash. Now you have a reasonable idea if you let God do it through you or you don't. God won't reward what He didn't do. That's how the cookie crumbles.

Pugh proverb: "It's hard to live the Christian life, but it's harder on you not to."

Scripture verses: Matthew 16:24–26; Luke 16:19–31, 15:11–24; 2 Corinthians 11:23–33; 2 Timothy 4:6–8; 1 Corinthians 2:9; 2 Timothy 3:12

Most people believe that when they come to Christ for salvation, all their problems will be over. That's the sales pitch that's given. You are told of a loving God who will answer all your prayers. You will have peace and happiness from then on. God will remove all troubles from your life and then take you to heaven to be with Him forever when you die. It sounds too good to be true. Who wouldn't want such a life? Though the claim of a wonderful life provided by a relationship with a God who loves you is completely true, there is another part of the Christian life that includes pain, difficulties, and suffering.

Second Timothy 3:12 tells us "all that will live godly in Christ Jesus shall suffer persecution." According to statistics given by the Institute for the Defense of the Persecuted Church, over 250,000,000 Christians worldwide suffer daily persecution. It should come as no surprise that Satan hates a Christian and is going to come at them to stop them from being used by God to win others to Christ. He wants us to appear as fools for trusting in Jesus. He wants people to believe it's not worth it. Satan wants to paint us as hypocrites that will crack under the pressure he puts upon us.

This world's system is no friend to the Christian. It wants to erode our commitment to Christ. Taking a stand against the world, the flesh, and the devil is hard. I'll give you an example out of my own life. When I was in the ninth grade, I was elected student body president. Little did I know the difficulty that would bring into my life during the school year.

I was sitting in my English class during second period when I heard my name being called over the intercom. "Dwane Pugh, report to the principal's office immediately," squawked the intercom overhead. As I left the room and made my way toward the principal's office, I tried to imagine what I had or had not done to be called in. I couldn't think of any crimes I had committed…lately, so I entered his office not knowing what to expect.

Mr. Holland, the school's principal, was a stately looking gentleman of about sixty-five years of age. The gray hair around his temples spoke symbolically of the wisdom of the man, acquired from being the school's principal for over thirty years. He had been at the school during the years my three older brothers had come through the educational system and was well acquainted with my family.

"Dwane, sit down. We have somewhat of a situation here. Because of budget restraints, we are going to cancel the spring formal dance planned for next Friday. Word of this has leaked out, and the other ninth-grade class has staged a sit-in in their first-period class." You have to remember, this was the seventies and sit-ins were a common way for people to put pressure on leaders to get what they wanted.

He acknowledged, "I could come up with the money from other sources."

Then what's the problem? I thought.

"However, we have been getting reports of serious misconduct happening at past dances. I don't have enough teachers to supervise these events properly. I can't risk that type of activity happening again."

"If I may ask, sir, what kind of problems?"

Mr. Holland looked sad as he answered the question. "Students have been making out in the locker rooms. Some have been smoking

pot outside or doing other drugs. At times, fights have broken out."
After a pause, Mr. Holland asked, "Are you planning on coming to
the dance?"

The question caught me off guard. "No, sir, I am not. You know
my mother doesn't believe in letting us go to dances. Why do you
ask?"

What he said next floored me. "I need someone I can trust who
would be around the students without rousing suspicion before and
during the dance. They could hear what was going on and report
anything questionable to me. If you will come to the dance and do
that, then we will have it. If you don't, I can't risk it, and the dance
will remain canceled."

"I need to talk with my mother before I can give you an answer,
sir," was my reply. He nodded and said I could return to class. As I
walked back toward my class, I was in a daze. How could he put me
in this situation? If I didn't agree to go and people found out I was
the reason we weren't having the dance, I would ruin my ability to
reach them for Christ or to influence other Christians at school. If I
did agree to go, would I be going against God by giving into pressure
and compromising the standards taught me by my godly mother?

Not seconds after I walked back into my English class and sat
down, a girl from across the next row of seats whispered, "Have you
decided yet?"

"How do you know about it already?" was my reply.

"I was in the secretaries' office running an errand for the teacher
and overheard."

*If this girl already knows, it's going to be all over the school as soon
as this period ends* was the thought that kept running through my
mind the remainder of the class.

I didn't know what I was going to do. As I mused over it the rest
of the day, I was solaced by the fact my mother would never agree to
it. She would then become the bad guy, and I could blame not having the dance on her. I could then retain my respected status as a cool
guy at school and still not incur the wrath of God for compromising.
It seemed to be the light at the end of the tunnel, the answer to all
my problems.

It was not. When I came home and told mom about the situation, she did the most unexpected thing she could do. She gave me the power to decide for myself what God would have me do. Mom believed it was time for me to be led by God without her giving me instructions. She would pick now, of all times, to start giving me this freedom. I was between a rock and a hard place, and I knew it. Hour after hour, I agonized over the matter, praying hard for the answer.

It was my habit to walk in the dark at night when praying. As I looked up at the stars and asked God for the wisdom I needed, He reminded me He had designed me for this moment and this set of circumstances. Peace flooded my soul as I thought about this wonderful truth. Honoring Him and reaching others with His love were the two goals that became crystal clear in my mind, guiding my thoughts. Now I had the plan that would free me from this no-win situation.

The next morning at school, I went straight to Mr. Holland's office and informed him I would be at the dance if he would approve having it. He went back over the secret mission he wanted me to perform, and I indicated I would do the job. No one knew about that part, so when Mr. Holland made the announcement the spring dance was on again, I became an instant hero. People were coming up to me, thanking me for making the dance possible. I must admit, that felt good.

The day of the dance had come, and it was now time to implement phase two of the plan God had given me. I came to the dance an hour before others could get in the gymnasium where the dance was being held. I scoped out the area and found nothing suspicious hidden in the gym. The teachers would do the rest by checking each student for anything illegal as they came in. As people arrived, they found me sitting in a corner, reading my Bible. When it became too dark for me to read by the light coming in the gym windows, I just sat and watched the goings on of people dancing and talking.

Nothing seemed to be amiss. I did note the music was too loud and too questionable for my taste and how funny some people were when they danced. However, every once in a while, someone who really did know how to dance would put on a show for all who were watching. I felt I was honoring God as I mildly enjoyed myself. Then, it happened. A girl I had liked since the third grade came over and asked me to dance.

What was I going to do? I had been taught dancing could very easily lead to lust and to avoid it at all cost. As a teenage boy, I knew what raging hormones were like. I could only imagine how hard it would be to keep my thoughts straight as our bodies moved in close contact with each other. I did so want to hold this girl in my arms and win her heart. I wanted to look deep into her eyes and see if there was any romantic interest in me.

What I chose to do was one of the hardest things I had ever done at that point in my life. I told her as a Christian, I didn't dance, though I didn't condemn others for doing so. Amazingly so, she begged me to dance with her just this one time. Though weakened, my resolve held firm. In a last-ditch effort to dance with me, she sent my cousin over to try to talk me into it. I refused to reconsider, and the opportunity was gone forever.

I may have lost a romantic memory in that moment, but God has blessed me with an amazing godly wife and family. Very few marriages and families have enjoyed what God has built into mine. I would not trade the sadness and pain of that moment for the blessings of God on my life. Too many people chase dreams only to find out the reality is not worth the effort. The easy path leads to places that can't stand the test of time.

The Apostle Paul knew of the challenges of living the Christian life. He writes in 2 Corinthians 11:23–33.

> Are they ministers of Christ? (I speak as a fool) I am more; in labors more abundant; in stripes above measure, in prisons more frequent, in peril of death, often. Of the Jews five times received I thirty nine lashes with a whip. Three times was I beaten with rods, once was I stoned, three times I suffered shipwreck, a night and a day I have been set adrift in the sea; On frequent journeyings, in danger in the water, in danger of robbers, in

> danger by my own countrymen, in danger by the
> Gentiles, in danger in the city, in danger in the
> wilderness, in danger in the sea, in danger among
> false brothers; In weariness and painfulness, in
> toil and hardship often, in hunger and thirst, in
> fastings often, in cold and exposure.

Did Paul think it was worth it? I will let him answer you in his own words found in Romans 8:18. "For I consider that the sufferings of this present time are not worthy to be compared with the glory which will be revealed in us." Jesus gives us a warning concerning satisfaction in this life. "For whoever will save his life will lose it: and whoever will lose his life for my sake will find it" (Matthew 16:25). Abundant life is found in walking with God no matter how hard the path may seem.

I have observed this in my own family. I have a brother who was brought up with the same parents and upbringing I was. However, he got away from the Lord as a young teenage through experimenting with ESP (extrasensory perception). He tried to learn how to make things happen through his mind's power to manipulate his circumstances. ESP was big in the sixties and seventies. People bent spoons with their minds and manipulated objects. All sorts of things were tried by people.

Little did he know, it was by demonic power these things were done. Satan used ESP to cloud his mind, making him think there were better ways than trusting God to have a great life. Though saved, he tapped into other spiritual forces that led him down a dark path of destruction. As a young married man studying to be a minister, he had a mental breakdown that began years of pain and heartache.

He has been in an out of mental institutions over the years. He lost his family, with his wife divorcing him and his daughter not ever wanting to see him again. Two other marriages failed. He spent ten years living in homeless shelters, owning nothing but the clothes he was wearing. When he would turn to the Lord, his life would take an upturn as God blessed his obedience. He helped a senator from North Carolina craft groundbreaking legislation for mental health laws that became a model for other states. He became a sought-after speaker on the subject of mental health, winning several state awards and was on multiple mental health boards.

Then pride and self-reliance would creep back in, and down his life would go. His life has been a testimony to the Pugh proverb, "It's hard to live the Christian life but it's harder on you not to." Currently, he is doing well. He is finishing up his masters' degree in mental health and is going to pursue his doctorate. My brother recently shared with me he has never been in a better place with God. Surrender to God's control has brought joy, peace, and contentment to his soul.

Challenges, difficulties, pain, and suffering sooner or later come to us all. It is the choices we make and who we turn to that defines us and brings us to a place of blessing in this life or the next. The story of the rich man and Lazarus from Luke 16 illustrates this fact.

The rich man seemingly had a wonderful life. He "faired sumptuously every day." That means he ate very well. He wore the finest clothes, lived in a big house, and had plenty of servants to do his bidding. In his own family and in the community, he was a leader. Lazarus, however, was a different story. He was a beggar who sat by the rich man's gate. He was physically suffering through starvation and sores all over his body. His only consolation was dogs licking his sores.

Both men died at the same time. The rich man went to an eternal damnation of fire, but Lazarus went to a place of unimaginable bliss. The rich man was told, "Remember that thou in thy lifetime received thy good things and likewise Lazarus evil things: but now he is comforted and thou art tormented" (Luke 16:25). Choices they made concerning God and others forged their futures. It's the same with us.

Someone may say, "It's too hard to be a Christian. I don't want to have to give up my current lifestyle to become a Christian." As someone who has accepted Christ as Savior, nothing could be further from the truth. All you have to do is acknowledge you are a sinner and can't do anything good enough to take away your sin. Next, believe Jesus is the only sacrifice for your sin problem with God and that He arose from the dead for you. Lastly, surrender yourself to Him. Tell Him you don't want to be a rebel against Him but have a personal relationship with Him as ruler of your life.

It is so easy, a child can do it. Your new eternal life can start today if you pray and tell God these things. I am not promising a life in this world without challenges, but the love of a heavenly Father who can turn bad into good and will someday take you to an eternal existence is so wonderful, you can't imagine it. The choice is yours. But remember, it's hard to live the Christian life, but it's harder on you not to.

Application

I love object lessons. This application has to do with an object lesson that I hope will drive home this Pugh proverb. Pick out a course of about half a mile that you can walk. If possible, include some terrain that will challenge you during the walk. Take a walk on your trail. Time yourself if you like. The next day, fill a backpack with weights, rocks or sand, anything heavy.

Now with the backpack on, take a walk on the same path as the day before. During or after the walk, think about the difference between the walks in time and effort. Then, mentally list the things in your life that are extremely hard and ask yourself this honest question: "Am I making my life harder than it has to be by not obeying God?"

Pugh proverb: "The greatest gift you can give God is to trust Him in the dark."

Scripture verses: Romans 4:3, 18–21; Romans 8:24–25; Hebrews 11:1, 6, 8

Fear of the unknown is one of the most powerful fears in a person's life. You struggle to find a reference point of reality to guide your response to different situations. If you have a known enemy, you can fight it. However, if you don't know what or where the enemy is, it's hard to feel safe. Problems are easier to solve if you know what they are and their causes. You can prepare for situations you see coming, but preparing for every possible danger will drive a person mad. It can't be done.

That is why I trust an unknown future to a known God. Because of a personal relationship with God through Christ's atoning death and resurrection, I know God's character. God can't cease to be who He is. He is truth and thus cannot lie. God doesn't just have love, He is perfect love. He is all-powerful, all-knowing, and everywhere at one time. He never leaves you nor forsakes you. He does not change because He is perfect. If you believe these truths, your actions and attitudes will demonstrate you can trust God in the darkest moments in your life.

I have endeavored to teach the concept of faith to my children. When you read how I chose to do this, you may think me to be a bad parent, but my children have all thanked me for the object lesson.

They have given testimony of how it has helped them in their own dark times.

As babies in their crib at night, I would lay on the floor beside them with my hand reaching up to hold theirs until they fell asleep. I would do this until I could see they understood the pattern. Months later, my next step was to not hold their hand but just lay beside the crib on the floor. They would call out, "Daddy, are you still there?" I would immediately answer them, assuring them I was not going anywhere.

Once they became consistently comfortable with that pattern, I explained I wanted them to trust me and would not be answering them when they asked if I was still there. Their little heads would pop up to see if I was really there when they called out and I didn't answer. I would remind them daddy will be there for them because that's what I promised. They should trust my word and faithfulness, not their own thoughts or feelings. Until they could go to sleep without asking if I was still there, I continued the object lesson. The next step was to sleep out in the hall with a light on so they could see me. I was not in the room but was able to watch over them. They were still safe in daddy's care.

The process took a couple of years, depending on each child's ability to be comfortable with the situation. When they were ready, I would graduate to taking them into a dark room with me holding their hand. The same promise of being there for them was reinforced. We would spend a couple of minutes in the room and then emerge to talk about the experience. "Did you know daddy was there for you in the dark?"

"Yes, I could feel your hand in mine," was usually their response.

"Okay, but daddy wants you to trust he is there because he promised he would be, not because you can make sure of it on your own."

In time, I would not hold their hand when we entered the dark room but would answer when they called. The next phase of the lesson was to reaffirm my promise of being there to keep them safe but explain I would not touch them or answer when they called. Without fail, each one after a couple of minutes would ask if I was still there.

Upon getting no response, they would search for me, groping in the dark. Unless I detected deep fear setting in, I would silently evade them until they gave up.

I always went back over the lessons that should have been learned and their present response to the situation. My desire for them to trust a promise I had given them once as iron clad was my goal. When we were able to stay for over five minutes in the dark without any fear, I ended the process. At the end, I explained, "If you can trust an imperfect father in the dark, you definitely can trust your heavenly Father when you don't understand things happening in your life."

We see that kind of faith exhibited by Abraham. Hebrews 11:8–9 recounts the story of God's promise to Abraham and his journey "in the dark."

"By faith Abraham, when he was called to go out into a place which he should, in time received for an inheritance, obeyed; and he went out, not knowing where he was going. By faith he lived as an outsider in the land of promise, as in a foreign country; dwelling in tents with Isaac and Jacob, the heirs with him of the same promise."

Romans 4:3 states, "Abraham believed God, and God counted it for him as righteousness." Abraham displayed in his life a pattern of trusting God. God promised Abraham and Sarah a son but waited decades before He would deliver on that promise.

Romans 4:18–21 puts it this way: "Who against hope believed in hope, that he might become the father of many nations, according to that which was fortold, So shall your offspring be. And being not weak in faith, he considered not his own body now past childbearing years, when he was about an hundred years old, neither yet the barrenness of Sarah's womb. He staggered not at the promises of God through unbelief; but was strong in faith, giving glory to God; And being fully persuaded that, what he had promised, he was able also to perform."

As a youth pastor for over thirty years, I have taught concepts about faith to many teenagers. One of my favorite ways of doing this is to take them on what I call a faith walk. Usually after a cookout and some fun activities, when it was dark enough, I would announce we would be taking a faith walk as part of our devotional lesson. "What's a faith walk?"

"You'll see," was my response to their question.

I would instruct them to line up single file, close enough to touch the shoulder of the person in front of them. After telling them to put their hand on the shoulder of the person in front of them, I would get to the front of the line with someone's hand on my shoulder and start off walking in the dark. Someone would always call out, "Where are we going?"

"I know, but you don't need to know to get to where you need to be. All you have to do to safely arrive at the right destination is to maintain contact with the person in front of you, who is connected to people in front of them, who are connected to me. I am quite capable of travelling this path in the dark."

That was a true statement. As already mentioned, I love to walk in the dark at night and pray. The prayer path I usually walked was about half a mile. It took me over a paved road to an old logging road to a narrow footpath, leading to the dam at the back side of Lake Orange. The terrain varied greatly, and the path took many twists and turns. I sometimes had to avoid fallen tree trunks and overhanging limbs to safely make it through. I, however, had made the journey hundreds of times, many of them in the dark.

The teens would have varied reactions to the journey. Some would become fearful and want to go back. Others would try to play off their uneasiness by making jokes and lots of noise. Many times that cost them an unpleasant moment by not heeding my warnings about upcoming dangers ahead. Every once in a while, someone would lose contact with the person in front of them and become disoriented. They would get off the path and become momentarily lost. Calling out for help, they would get reconnected and continue the journey.

When we arrived back at my home, I would ask them about the experience. Very few said they were at peace while in the dark. They didn't like the feeling of being out of control. Of the ones who said they were at peace during the walk, trust in me and staying focused on what I had told them to do was the reason given for their calm.

They knew I cared about them and would not lead them into harmful situations. Confidence in my ability to safely navigate the dangers made the lesson fun and powerful for them.

Hebrews 11:1 says, "Now faith is the assurance of things hoped for, the evidence of things not seen." You can experience the reality of something by knowing that if God says it is real, it is real. If God says a certain choice path leads to a certain destination, it does. If God says something is going to happen, it will.

According to Hebrews 11:6, you can't please God without faith. "But without faith, it is impossible to please him; for he that cometh to God must believe that he is, and is a rewarder of them that diligently seek him."

Another Bible character who understood this principle is Joseph. His real life story is told in chapters thirty-seven through fifty of the book of Genesis. God gives Joseph a dream as a youth, promising amazing blessings in the future. However, the journey to the fulfillment of that promise is filled with dark times. His brothers hated him for his dream and planned to kill him but sold him as a slave instead. Joseph is sold in Egypt to a man named Potiphar who is the captain of pharaoh's guard. His wife lies about being attacked by Joseph when he refuses her sexual advancements, and is thrown into prison.

While in prison, he interprets the dream of two of pharaoh's top servants. The one who was restored to his former position promises to tell pharaoh of Joseph's unjust punishment for a crime he didn't commit. He did not. Joseph spends years in prison before God delivers him in a most miraculous way. During all the dark years of not knowing what God was doing or why He was doing it, Joseph did not stop obeying and following God. He just kept doing the most God-honoring thing he could do in the situations he faced.

Because of his faith, God elevated Joseph to the pinnacle of power in Egypt and the known world at that time. He saved the nation of Egypt and the Jewish race. His own words in Genesis 50:20 reveal his understanding of the reward of trusting God in the dark. "But as for you, you thought evil against me; but God meant it unto good, to bring to pass, as it is this day, to save many people alive."

I have had to trust God in the dark many times in my life. One of those times has to do with my current situation. I am the founding pastor of Abundant Life Christian Fellowship in Orange, Virginia. It is a wonderful country church of about 225 people who call it home. How I got here is a story of walking in the dark.

Twenty-five years ago, I was serving in a church in North Carolina as assistant pastor and music and youth director. The church also had a Christian school at which I was the assistant high school principal, taught seventh through twelfth grade Bible, and was a coach and athletic director. Needless to say, I was a busy man. The Lord was blessing the ministry I was doing there. Because of that, I didn't expect what He told me one day during my devotions. Out of the blue, God told me He was ending up my ministry there in the near future and would be moving me somewhere else. He didn't say when or where.

Two events dictated the when. The Christian school I was at had just hired a new high school principal. He was from up north and was not accustomed to our southern ways of doing things. In his first three months, he had created through his abrasive ways enough problems that there were calls for his termination as principal. I was assigned the task of putting out the fires he had created until he could adjust.

One day during a meeting with the pastor concerning the behavior of a student, the principal dropped a bombshell. I was about to give my take on the situation when he said, "Stop right there. I don't want to hear a thing you have to say. Your way of doing things and mine are too different, and sooner or later, one of us will have to leave." It was a bold thing to say considering the pastor was my older brother with whom I had worked successfully for nineteen years.

"Then I guess it will have to be me," was my reply. I then turned to my brother and gave my resignation. The principal began to do some hard backpedaling, but my brother knew me well enough to know I had not made the decision out of rash emotion. He did, however, ask that I tell no one, not even my wife, until the semester break at Christmas. That would hopefully give the principal enough time to gain some support before the shocking news was released. I would finish out the school year and then leave.

The second event signaling the when was the news that my wife was pregnant with our third child. This announcement came a few weeks after I had secretly resigned. As a father, I had made a commitment to spend one hour each day with each of my children. With the demands of the ministry, I had no more time to give. I was putting my family to bed and then staying up until past midnight to prepare for the next day. With a third child on the way, I didn't see how I could continue in the current ministry without compromising my principles as a father or the quality of the ministry. Finding out we were about to have another baby confirmed the decision God had led me to make.

Now it was time to seek God for the where. After I had told my wife of the decision at Christmas break, we began to pray earnestly for God's direction in the process. I had no desire to have multiple offers on the table. That might give Satan the opportunity to get me to take a ministry on the basis of what was best for me rather than God's call to that ministry. I asked God to allow me to pursue one opportunity at a time. Until that door had closed or was stuck in a holding pattern, I would only pursue that ministry possibility. If a door did close or was in a holding pattern, I would move on to consider the next opportunity.

In each of the first two ministry opportunities, I was the first candidate they had brought in to consider. I would preach a great sermon, or so I was told, and have a wonderful interview. Each time, the pulpit committee would indicate I was their desire for the job, but they still needed to go through the process with the other candidates. When I came to the third option, I was sure it was not going to be something that would work out.

There were three reasons why I believed this to be true. One is they were not Independent Baptist in theology and I was. Two is that it was a group of eight people who had been hurt recently in a church who wanted to start one. I never wanted to start a church. The final reason was no salary would be possible for some time until the group grew to the size that could provide one. I did go and meet with them, confident I was only doing due diligence to the process God had approved.

Upon talking with them, I could see they were in need of some spiritual healing. They loved the Lord and wanted solid Bible teaching and didn't care about denominational labels. During the four-and-a-half-hour drive back to my house, God stirred my heart to consider their need.

In the coming days, I sought counsel from a few pastor friends of mine. Each one indicated if God would let them, they would prefer to pastor a new church. There would be no strange church traditions to fight and no stubborn power structure in place to win over to the pastor's leadership. Basically, there would be no skeletons in the closet to deal with.

Though still greatly struggling, I was seeing more and more indicators that God was leading me to start that church. The last straw happened during a Sunday morning worship service. My brother was preaching. He had us turn to a certain scripture verse he was about to explain. I had just prayed that God would show me something in His word to lead me in my decision. It was not that verse but another verse on the opposite side of the page that drew my attention to it like a magnet.

"Jesus was led by the Spirit into the Wilderness to be tested by the devil." The area in Orange, Virginia, where they wanted to start the church was less than ten miles from a battlefield called Wilderness Battlefield. You may think it bizarre, but I knew God had just told me to go to the "wilderness" and start a church. I had so many unanswered questions, but I was determined to follow God's leading into the dark.

No one thought I was doing the right thing. They would point to the effective ministry I was doing and indicate its need to continue. Family would talk about my responsibility to my newborn son, the lack of future income, and all the current benefits I would be giving up to go to Virginia and start a church. They posed questions for which I had no answers. Based on the first year living in Virginia, it looked like they were right and I was out of God's place of blessing.

The first year was a nightmare of things not going as planned. Within three months, three of the four founding families had left the church. The land my in-laws had given us upon which to build a house would not perk. The soil was too poor to sustain a septic system. Our house in North Carolina would not sell. As we searched for other housing options, we discovered the cost of living was much higher in Virginia. We would have to borrow money to buy or build a smaller house than we had in North Carolina.

For fifteen months, my wife and three children lived in two bedrooms in my in-laws' house, which also served as the church's meeting place. On four different occasions during that first year, my wife broke under the pressure. She accused me of being out of God's will, saying I had only come to Virginia to please her by being near her parents.

In the second half of the year, we moved to an old community building called a Grange Hall. We shared it with the coon hunters who used it as their headquarters for weekend hunts. They didn't see any problem with keeping their dogs inside at night because of the run-down condition of the building. It was cold in the winter and hot in the summer. During one service in January, a cup of water on the podium froze solid by the time I finished preaching. The temperature would be in excess of ninety degrees at the end of the service during the midsummer months.

It truly was a dark time. Strange as it may seem, I never doubted I was obeying God. He was at work in ways I could not see. My job was to trust and obey. He would take care of results in His own time, and He did. Over the twenty-five years the church has been in existence, multiple hundreds of people have come to know Christ as Savior. Families have been restored. Christians have grown in the grace and knowledge of God. Miracles of healing, both physical and mental, have taken place. God has done and is doing a work that justifies His leading me here, even if it was in the dark.

I will never forget what God told me one time as I was meditating on His sovereign purposes in everything. I was watching some insects flying over a green field. "You know I have placed every blade of grass the way it is now to affect things hundreds of years into the future. Do you really want me to explain it all to you? Do you think you could take it all in? See those insects. I am adjusting the wind with their wing's movement to affect weather around the world. Do you need to know all the whys of my work?"

"No. It would blow my mind. I'll just trust you and enjoy the day," was my response.

Romans 8:24–25 says, "We are saved by hope: but hope that is seen is not hope; for what a man sees, why does he yet hope for it? But if we hope for what we see not, then do we with patience wait for it." For me and many others, God has earned the right to be trusted in the dark. He sees just.

Application

This is a fun way to apply this proverb. I have used this to illustrate it many times. You will need to create an obstacle course using chairs, boxes, or orange cones. Anything that is moveable and will not hurt someone if they bumped into it can be used. Make a maze requiring left-and-right movement to avoid obstacles. You can even make it where you have to move at an angle.

One person will be blindfolded and be directed to go through the maze. The other person will use voice commands to help them to do so. You can even make it fun by putting a prize like money or candy on a table at the end of the maze. If a person touches an obstacle, they lose. You can try again or change places and play the game.

It teaches you to trust the one who can see to help you through the maze and not your own perception. Just like in real life, you will have to deal with confusion, fear, doubt, and frustration as how to move forward. You and your helper will have to become a team for you to succeed.

9

Pugh proverb: "God is fair, even with the devil."

Scripture verses: Job 1–2:7; Matthew 4:1–11; Galatians 6:7–8; Proverbs 14:34; 1 Corinthians 5:1–5

The majority of people in the world believe there is a cosmic battle going on between good and evil. You may be one of them. You believe these opposites are locked in a conflict to decide what force will determine the fate of all things. Nothing could be further from the truth. God is all-powerful. Nothing takes place without His allowance. However, God plays by His own rules. For men and angels to truly have a free will, they must be allowed to make choices opposite of God's desire. God will never allow a choice to be made that, if placed in His hands, will not work out to a person's benefit. The battle is over what will be chosen, not who is in control. The appearance that evil is winning is only an illusion.

This can be seen in the life of Job. If you read the first two chapters of Job, you will see what I mean. Job was an amazing guy. God said so Himself in the very first verse. Job was "perfect and upright, and one that feared God and eschewed [stayed away from] evil." Because of his obedience, God had greatly blessed Job. In verse six and following of the first chapter, we get a rare look into the spirit world concerning a conversation between God and Satan.

> And the Lord said unto Satan, Where are you coming from? Then Satan answered the Lord, and said, From going back and forth in the earth,

and from walking up and down in it. And the Lord said unto Satan, Have you considered my servant Job, that there is none like him in the earth, a perfect and an upright man, one that fears God, and hates evil? Then Satan answered the Lord, and said, Does Job fear God for nothing? Have you not made a hedge of protection around him, and around his house, and all that he has on every side: you have blessed the work of his hands, and his material possessions are increased in the land. But take your hand of blessing away now, and touch all that he has, and he will curse you to your face. (Job 1:7–11)

If Job had known what was going on, I am sure he would have asked God to not mention him before Satan. Satan had just come from surveying the earth to seek out people he could control and torment. God rubs Job's godliness in Satan's face as someone he could not get to. Satan argues that the only reason Job obeys God is that God protects and blesses him. He believes Job's motivation is self-serving and not from a desire to surrender to God.

God is fair with the devil and gives him an opportunity to prove his point. "And the Lord said unto Satan, Behold, all that he hath is in thy power, only upon himself put not forth thine hand. So Satan went forth from the presence of the Lord." Satan then makes Job's life a living hell. In the space of less than twenty-four hours, Job loses everything. His children are killed by a tornado collapsing a building upon them and three different groups of raiders kill his servants and take all his livestock away. He goes from the penthouse to the outhouse just like that. Amazingly so, Job does not sin or bad-mouth God.

Not one to quit, Satan meets with God again and discusses Job. Once again, God rubs Job's obedience, even in the light of God allowing Satan to attack him, in Satan's face. Satan answers God, "Skin for skin, yea, all that a man hath will he give for his life. But put forth thine hand now, and touch his bone and his flesh, and he will curse thee to thy face. And the Lord said unto Satan, Behold, he is in thine hand; but save his life."

Because God is fair even with the Devil, round two of Job's torture begins. Satan causes a skin disorder, producing pain, itching, and runny sores from the top of his head to the bottom of his feet. It's so bad, Job takes broken pieces of pottery and scrapes his flesh constantly, trying to stop the itching. As someone who has occasionally had itches that wouldn't stop no matter how I scratched them, it can be maddening.

You may be asking why God would allow Satan to do such things to Job. It is because a faith that cannot be tested should not be trusted. Satan is trying to prove God to be wrong and his servants to be phonies. God must display His truth for all to see by giving Satan the opportunity to attack it. My own life has been given over to Satan at times to be fairly tested.

One example of this comes from my childhood and teenage years. A cycle of deep, dark depression would come over me for no apparent reason. Nothing would be amiss in my life circumstances or walk with the Lord that should cause such a cloud of evil. A lot of times, things would actually be going better than normal. The darkness would never last more than three days. Praying and Bible reading and study would not take it away during that time.

I would seek solitude in the deep woods or night darkness and just sit before the Lord. There would be an ache in my soul for God, but I couldn't seem to sense His presence. I came to realize in my later years of life that it was a garden-of-Gethsemane moment. Jesus was attacked that way the night of His betrayal before His crucifixion. Just as there was a resurrection Sunday, I would be resurrected in time to my normal spiritual and mental state. I was being tested because God is fair even with the devil.

Jesus was "led by the Spirit to be tempted by the Devil" at the beginning of His earthly ministry according to Matthew 4:1. Men and angels needed to see Jesus as the God-man who could take the best or worst Satan could throw at Him and still emerge triumphant. Satan took his best shot and lost. Jesus is who He claims to be. God being fair with Satan to test that claim ended up proving it.

Not all open doors given to Satan are because of the godliness of the person being tested. More often, it is the result of the biblical principle of sowing and reaping. Galatians 6:7–8 states, "Be not deceived; God is not mocked by being proven wrong: for whatever a man sows by his actions, that will he also reap. For whoever sows to his flesh shall of the flesh reap corruption; but he that sows to the Spirit will of the Spirit reap life everlasting." God warns that you open a doorway in your life for Satan to attack when you violate God's commands.

An Old Testament example of this is found in 1 Chronicles 21:1–30. King David, because of pride and fear in his mind concerning the strength of his army, commanded that the number of fighting men be recorded. According to verse one, "Satan stood up against Israel and provoked David to number Israel." Satan knew if he could get David to sin, he would have the right to attack Israel. In response to David's disobedience, verse seven says, "And God was displeased with this thing; therefore he smote Israel." You need to not forget that God allows Satan's work to be His chastening tool to bring people back to a place of blessing. Satan is not winning, but he is at work.

Before I give some personal examples, let me give you a New Testament example of God being fair with the devil. First Corinthians 5:1–5 is Paul's response to the question of how to deal with an individual's sin in the church at Corinth. A man in the church was having sexual relationship with his stepmother. Paul advises in verse five to "deliver such a one over to Satan for the destruction of the flesh that the spirit may be saved at the day of Jesus Christ." The Bible does not record if the man repented or not. If he did not, for the rest of his life, Satan would be allowed to tear his life apart.

As a pastor for many years, I have seen the disobedience of countless individuals cause the ills of their lives. Instead of giving other people's stories, I will share two from my own life. It concerns the first girl with which I was ever in love. I had been dating this girl for about two years; and over time, she had become the source of my happiness, the person I most wanted to please.

God had been warning me in various ways for about six months that I was making this girl an idol in my life. He gave me chances to repent and return to a rightful balance in my affections for her, but I wouldn't listen. Satan had convinced me it was easier to turn to a visible person to make my life worth living than to an invisible God. Had I known what Satan was going to be allowed to do in my life, I hope I would have had the good sense to break out of his spell through heartfelt repentance.

A week after God's final warning, we were playing in a National Invitational Basketball Tournament for Christian high schools sponsored by Tennessee Temple University. It was the semifinals. We were the number-one seed playing the number-two seed. We were evenly matched, and it was a back-and-forth game. With less than two minutes to go and nursing a one-point lead, my coach called on me to run the four corners. For those of you who do not know basketball, the four corners is when you possess the ball by holding onto it by dribbling and passing the ball without necessarily trying to score.

I was the main ball handler at that time and was doing a masterful job of running it. The other team was unable to steal the ball from me, and with time running down to the last ten seconds, they were forced to foul me. If I hit both free throws, the game would be over. This was before the three-point shot was instituted into basketball. If I just hit one, we could not lose but could be tied and then go into overtime.

To set the stage for what was about to happen, let me say that in the free throw drill the day before, I hit twenty out of twenty-five free throws. That's 80 percent. The other coach called time out, trying to rattle me into missing at least one of the free throws. As I went to the bench, I was supremely confident. This was my time to shine as a senior and be the hero. Our coach encouraged me to remain calm, reminding me I was a good free throw shooter.

Upon returning to the court, the official gave me the ball and reminded everyone, "Two shots." I went through my usual rhythm, bouncing the ball three times and then let it fly. I can still to this day see it in my mind's eye. It hit the front of the rim, the backboard, the side of the rim, and out. Immediately, the other coach called another time-out. I was a little shaken but believed I would hit the next shot. My coach had a little more intensity in his voice when he said, "We really need you to make this shot."

I stepped up to the free throw line, and the ball was placed in my hand. "One shot," the referee called out.

"Dear God, please help me make this shot," I silently prayed. It was a carbon copy of the last shot: front of the rim, backboard, side of the rim, and out. The other team got the rebound and called time-out. I walked back to our bench in a daze. How could this happen to me? To make matters worse, to my shame, the coach took me out of the game.

We still could win the game, I thought. What are the odds the other team can get it up the court under full court pressure and score? Not likely. Again, I prayed, and again, my prayer was answered with a resounding *no* from God. The ball was put into play. With two defenders on him, the other team's guard threw up a shot from half-court as the buzzer sounded. You guessed it. I can still see it in my mind's eye swishing the net for a one-point win for the other team.

This was just the beginning of the misery I had let into my life. Two weeks later, my girlfriend broke up with me, throwing me into a tailspin. For three weeks at night, I would complain to God for a couple of hours on how He had done me wrong. I reminded Him of all I had sacrificed for Him and how He not only didn't bless me in the basketball game but took away from me the thing I loved most. I felt the distance between God and me. It was like a darkness of soul I could physically feel.

After being silent for three weeks, letting me rail against Him, God spoke to my mind as clearly as any voice I could have heard with my natural ear. "Dwane, if you would put half the time and energy into your relationship with Me as you do in trying to get her back, you would find everything you're looking for in life and more. I tried to warn you, but you just wouldn't listen. You said it yourself. She is the thing you love most. Having an idol in your life is sin, and sin always releases a curse into your life." I learned that night that God is fair even with the devil.

Some lessons have to be repeated to be engrained into your soul. Plus, I can be hardheaded at times. This next life story is from my college days and has to do with basketball again. For years, the college basketball coach had tried to get me to go out for the team. I was working in a church as youth director and couldn't make doing that and playing in the games work out.

It was my last year in college, and they had hired a new basketball coach. I liked him and his style of basketball. After scoring thirty-three points in an intramural game, he asked me why my name wasn't on his list of players for the college. I explained the reason, but it didn't deter him. He asked me to pray about playing this year because he really wanted me on the team. I said I would, and I did. However, when I did, I ignored what God put on my heart as the answer. He had said no.

"That really can't be God," I reasoned. This was my last chance to play college basketball. God wouldn't take that away from me. After all, He was the one who gave me the talent to play well. I had sacrificed by not playing for three years to serve Him. Surely, it must be a false sense of duty and sacrifice that I am feeling. I used this line of thinking to cover up what I knew God had said.

I told the coach I would play for the team, and play I did…for two weeks. While playing in a basketball game, I stole the ball, ran down the court for a layup, and blew out my knee. It tore my ACL, LCL, and my meniscus. To this day, I still live with the consequences of knee pain for ignoring God. Though God has turned it all for good as I have repented and given it to Him, God was fair with the devil in allowing him to attack me this way. I know when I sin, I have released the devil into my life to kill, rob, and destroy because God is fair even with the devil.

I will give one more way God is fair even with the devil. God is a loving God and wants to give blessings to us but can't because we don't ask God in prayer for them. James 4:2 says we don't have because we don't ask. The following verses in James explain how our own lusts and the love of the world keep us at odds with God. We don't turn to Him, and thus, Satan prevents God from giving those blessings to us because he claims we don't want them. He is a master at using the fact of God being just to claim the right to attack us. We blame God for many of the problems in our world, but it's not His fault. Satan is at work. Don't fall into his trap because God will give the devil his due.

Application

Make a list of problems you see in the world, other people's lives, and your own. Get a Bible and look at Exodus 20:3–17. How many of the problems you have listed would not be a problem if the Ten Commandments were followed?

10

Pugh proverb: "Champions fight through a pain barrier others won't."

Scripture verses: 1 Samuel 16–17; 1 Samuel 31; 2 Samuel 23:8–39; 2 Corinthians 11:23–33

Talent is not the deciding factor that determines who is going to be a champion. Character that doesn't allow a person to quit when things are hard and a drive to give your very best, your all, determines it. I have coached a lot of different sports at all levels, except professionally, and have found this to be true. I have seen young kids with an abundance of talent choose to depend on natural ability to fuel their efforts and never rise to the level of their potential. I have also seen those with less talent dedicate themselves to getting better and, in time, surpass the player who initially had more talent.

This proverb is played out in our entertainment. We love to cheer for the underdog that goes through difficulties to win. Rocky is a good example. How many times have we seen him get beaten to a pulp and keep coming back for more? How many times have we watched him train in painful ways and felt an urge to cheer him on to victory? We vicariously identify with him, innately understanding the amazing character it takes to be a champion.

That is why I love the Olympics so much. When I consider the countless hours and sacrifices real people give to train day after day to compete at that level, it blows my mind. Some give four years of their life in training to compete, only to be beaten out of the medals by one-tenth of a second, and then do it all again for another four years in the hopes of being a champion.

It isn't just champion athletes that live by this principle. Our nation was birthed by people who lived out this truth. During the year of 1777, Washington and his army had known mostly defeat at the hands of the British. The British were so confident of victory, they chose to wait till spring to finish off the Colonials. They wintered in warm houses while Washington's forces wintered at Valley Forge.

It was a brutal winter. Conditions at Valley Forge were dire. Cold, hunger, and sickness plagued their bodies, while discouragement and doubt ate at their minds. Approximately two thousand troops died during those months. However, they did not quit. They believed their cause was just and the God of heaven would allow them to succeed in the end, and succeed they did. They built the greatest free nation the world has ever known. They were champions.

The Bible records the life of David in 1 and 2 Samuel, and we see this same kind of strength and character in him and his men. Though David was anointed by Samuel as the new king of Israel as a youth (1 Samuel 16), he did not come to reign until he had endured years of pain and difficulty. After David had killed Goliath (1 Samuel 17), King Saul became jealous of him and tried to kill him on multiple occasions.

David had to flee to enemy territory to escape Saul's reach. Over the next several years, David's life was in constant danger. Upon returning to his homeland, he lived in the caves of Israel, like an animal, to avoid capture by Saul. After King Saul's death (1 Samuel 31), Saul's son Ishbosheth waged civil war with David to claim the throne of Israel. Seven-and-a-half years later, David and his men prevailed and he was crowned king of a united Israel. Because of God's promise, he endured until he was victorious.

David attracted this same kind of character and perseverance in the men who followed him. In 2 Samuel 23:8–39, there is a list of David's mighty men. Thirty-three names of David's best soldiers are given. Of these thirty-three, three names stand out above the rest.

Examples of their exploits are given as evidence of their superior best-of-the-best status.

One of them is named Eleazar. During a battle against the Philistines, while other soldiers were running away, he stood his ground and fought. Listen to the biblical account. "He arose and smote the Philistines until his hand was weary and his hand clave [cramped] unto the sword: and the Lord wrought a great victory that day." At the end of the battle, they had to pry Eleazar's hand off the sword.

He would not let go until the battle was won. Now that's fighting through a pain barrier.

There are many more examples of this proverb found throughout the Bible. Paul is considered to be the greatest missionary of all time. What he went through to evangelize most of the known world at that time is recorded in 2 Corinthians 11:23–33, where Paul endured

> labours more abundant, in stripes above measure, in prisons more frequent, in deaths oft. Of the Jews five times I received thirty nine stripes. Three times I was beaten with rods, once was I stoned, three times I suffered shipwreck, a night and a day I have been adrift in the ocean; In travelling often, in danger in rivers, in dangers of robbers, in dangers by mine own countrymen, in danger by the heathen, in danger in the city, in danger in the wilderness, in danger in the sea, in danger among false believers; In weariness and painfulness, often in sleepless nights, in hunger and thirst, often fasting, in cold and nakedness.

That's quite a list making up the pain barrier Paul had to fight through to accomplish what he did. Though impressive, his is not the greatest pain barrier overcome to claim victory. Jesus bore and suffered for the sin of all mankind of all time when He died on the cross. The depth of what He went through can't be fathomed. He is the ultimate champion, and He did it all for you. He offers the free gift of eternal salvation to anyone who puts their trust in Him.

I have trusted Christ as my personal Savior and experienced His transforming power. He sets us free to be champions in our own lives. The question of releasing that victory into our own lives, once you have trusted Him as Savior, is will we be willing to fight through pain because we believe God has made us to succeed in life?

I know how hard that choice is. God has blessed me by making me a champion in many areas, but it came at a cost. I have won state and national championship tournaments in basketball. I was a state champion in Bible quiz team competitions. I have coached championship teams in soccer, basketball, and baseball. In my senior year in college, I was ranked tenth in the nation in the NCCAA for assists in soccer. I have been awarded coach of the year and assistant pastor of the year trophies during my lifetime.

It was not that I was more talented than others. It was that I understood three principles driving me past pain barriers others were unwilling to go through. First, success to the glory of God is worth it. Next, I must give my all. I check this by asking, "Do I have more to give? If so, then give it." Lastly, if I have surrendered my all to God to succeed, I am a champion. I perform for an audience of one—Jesus Christ. He gives me the strength to give my best, a championship effort that fights through the pain barriers of life.

Application

I encourage you to pick three people from history you admire and read a biography or autobiography about each person. You will find the things you admire about them have been forged in the fire of pain, difficulties, and hardship. If you don't like to read, pick three people with which you can converse and ask each to tell you about their life. You will come to the same conclusion. Champions in life fight through a pain barrier others won't.

11

Pugh proverb: "My sin is no problem to God; not bringing my sin to God is the problem."

Scripture verses: Genesis 3:8–14; Romans 6:12; Exodus 34:5–7; Proverbs 28:13

Have you ever done something wrong and tried to hide it? I believe everyone has at one time or another. If your experience is like mine, you've found out the hard way that the truth comes out sooner or later. I saw a video the other day with a little boy answering his mother's question concerning who ate the chocolate cookies. He indicated he did not and he didn't know who did. The problem was he had chocolate and cookie crumbs all over his face.

As a school bus driver, I have encountered the same thing on my bus route. Countless times I have witnessed a student throwing trash, eating on the bus, hitting someone, or switching seats while the bus is moving. When confronted, they deny it even though they know I was looking at them in the rearview mirror when they did it. Why do we try to hide our wrongdoings when it is so obvious we are guilty?

It is a part of our current spiritual DNA. It was not always so. According to the first two chapters of Genesis, God created mankind naked both physically and spiritually. Adam and Eve were honest with God as He came down each day to fellowship with them and were open and honest with each other. There was no reason to hide anything because they had not yet acquired the knowledge of good and evil.

Genesis 3:1–24 records how mankind acquired this knowledge and the awful consequences it entailed. God had given Adam and Eve only one rule: "Do not eat of the Tree of the Knowledge of Good and Evil. In the day you eat of it, you shall surely die." God did not want Adam and Eve to experience evil by becoming evil and thus be under God's righteous judgment. Adam and Eve's sinful choice changed their nature from innocence and goodness to deception and evil. They died spiritually the moment they defied God's protective command.

This is evidenced by their immediate desire to hide themselves from each other by making clothes of fig leaves. It also, in their minds, would allow them to camouflage their sinful state from God when He came down in the cool of the evening to fellowship with them. It did not. Though God did call out to Adam, "Where art thou?" as omniscient God, He knew where they were. He did so, so that Adam could see what sin had done to Him and Eve and come to Him for help.

Adam cites fear as the reason he was hiding. When God confronted him with his wrongdoing, instead of repenting of his sin, Adam blamed Eve for his sin, and God for giving him Eve by saying, "the woman which thou gave me." When God asked Eve about her giving Adam the forbidden fruit, she tried to hide her sin by blaming it on the serpent. It is a part of the fallen nature of mankind to not bring our sin to God for forgiveness but to hide it and, if confronted, blame others for it.

Note, however, it is God who makes a sacrifice to cover their sin even without being asked to do so. In symbolic nature, God portrays the Lamb of God, Jesus Christ, as the solution for mankind's sin when He kills a spotless lamb to cover their nakedness. However, mankind has a choice to make. God gives us a free will to accept His way of forgiveness or try to deal with our sin problem on our own. It is this knee-jerk reaction to run and hide from God that keeps us from experiencing His love and forgiveness.

Proverbs 28:13 says it this way. "He that covers his sin will not prosper but whoso confesses and forsake it shall have mercy." I have experienced the truth of this verse many times in my life. It is the basis of this particular proverb. Let me share just one of those occasions with you.

I was about twelve years old at the time. My oldest brother Adrian was a famous softball player in that area. He had been offered a contract out of high school to play baseball for the Saint Louis Cardinals but didn't accept it because of the death of my father and my being born at the same time. He was needed at home to help mom. So he turned his talents to playing on several industrial league softball teams in North Carolina.

He was going to be playing in our area and had offered to pick me up and take me to his game. The only problem was my mother and a friend of hers were going shopping, and I needed to stay home and entertain her son, Cecil. He was about my age, so I knew he liked softball. After some "creative negotiations," I had made the arrangement for me to ride home after the game with my brother and my friend's mother would come by the game after shopping to pick him up.

I was informed by my brother on the way to the game that it was a best-two-out-of-three games that determined the winner. That was fine with me. I loved being at the ballpark. I would always find some other young boys who wanted to go beyond the outfield fence and play cup ball. The game consisted of making a ball out of used paper cups and using your hands to hit it. After that, it was like regular baseball.

When my brother, who was nicknamed Big A, came to bat, the game always stopped. You see, if you returned a ball hit over the fence to the concessions stand, you would get a free drink. Big A almost always hit one over the fence, so every kid was ready for the mad dash to retrieve the ball. He was up to bat and delivered, as expected, a bomb over the center field fence. Cecil and I had positioned ourselves farther away from the fence, expecting such a bomb and were the first to get to the ball.

Upon delivering it to the concession stand to claim our prize, we found out the home run had ended the second game because of a slaughter rule. My brother met me at the stand and informed me it was time for us to leave. Cecil could stay and wait for his mother to pick him up because they were going to play the third game just for fun. I was disappointed. I was having a great time.

I whispered to Cecil, "Do you think your mother would take me home if I stayed?" It was out of her way, but he thought she would be glad to do so. Even though I knew it was a lie, I told my brother that mom had changed the plan and I would be riding home with my friend. He gave me a look and said, "Are you sure you have a ride?" I lied through my teeth with a smile on my face and said "yes."

We got our drink and headed back to the cup ball game. I watched my brother leave, confident everything would turn out all right even though I had lied. Not twenty minutes after the third game started, a heavy thunderstorm hit. We ran to take shelter under the awning of the concession stand. People began to leave because they had called off the rest of the game.

After about fifteen minutes, the only people who were left were those running the concession stand and us. They were wanting to leave and asked us if we needed a ride. I told them our ride would be along soon and we would just start walking toward home until they came to get us. Reluctantly, they said okay, and Cecil and I set out for my house. I had no real idea how far it was to my house. I guessed it was around six miles (I found out later, it was thirteen miles). It really didn't matter. Cecil's mom would be by soon and all would be well.

During the first fifteen minutes, three cars stopped and asked us if we needed a ride. Seeing two young teenagers walking in the rain brings out the best in people, especially in those days in rural North Carolina. Each time I told them no, sure that my plan would work out. It did not. We walked and walked and walked. For several hours, we walked. We hadn't seen a car since the first fifteen minutes after we left the ball field.

To make matters worse, it started raining harder again. I told Cecil, "This is all my fault. I never should have lied. I don't know what happened about your mother coming to get you, but I don't

76

think she is coming. We're going to have to find a house that will let us use their phone and call for help." That wasn't going to be easy. It was after eleven at night and no homes we passed had had lights on for a good while.

Finally, I was whipped. I knew I could not get myself out of this jam. I told Cecil we needed to stop and pray. He agreed. I prayed a simple prayer acknowledging my lying and my sinful pride. I asked God to forgive me and make a way to get me out of this nightmare. Within five minutes, we came upon a house with lights on. I reluctantly knocked on the door and backed up. I didn't want to get shot. I know how I would have felt if some stranger knocked on my door in the country at eleven thirty at night.

When the door opened, a man in a T-shirt and shorts about thirty years old looked us over and asked what we wanted. I explained the short version of our sad story. The ball game had been rained out, our ride didn't come for us, and we were trying to walk home. He chuckled as a look of pity for two drowned "rats" came over his face. He invited us in, and we made the call.

Both mothers were at my house and were still trying to track down what had happened to us. We found out they had cut their shopping off early because of the rain and had come by to pick us up. People were leaving, and upon not seeing us, they assumed my brother had taken us home with him and they left. When they called him, he didn't know where we were and relayed my made-up plan, my lie, to mom. She indicated they would be along to pick us up as soon as they could get there. I told her we would be walking because I didn't want to impose upon the family who had let us use the phone. She agreed and hung up.

As we walked, Cecil and I talked about our fate. We didn't think the hammer would fall on either of us until our mothers got us alone. At that point, we weren't sure what would happen. In about fifteen minutes, we saw headlights and got into the car. I felt like a criminal getting into the back seat of a police car as I closed the door. Our mothers asked if we were all right, but little more than that was said on the trip home. The silence was frightening.

77

After Cecil's mom let us out at home, mom told me to go take a warm bath, and after that, we would talk. As the chill left my body in the warm bathwater, a chill came over my soul. I replayed the whole sad tale in my mind and wondered how I could have been so stupid, so…sinful. I made things right with God and prepared to receive my just punishment. Before that "sentence" was given, I was sincerely going to ask my mother's forgiveness for lying (a great act of disrespect in my family) and making her worry.

As I entered the room after my bath, I began my heartfelt apology. After giving an honest account of my wrong and expecting the worst lecture of my life, plus some additional "corrective measures," she simply said, "Well, I figure you have suffered enough from your story. Did you learn your lesson?"

"Yes, ma'am," was my answer. That was the end of the matter. As I lay in bed thinking about it all, I realized how much my mother loved me, even when I am at my worst. She only wanted the best for me, and that was to be honest with myself and others before God and do right.

She learned that kind of love from her daily time spent with God. In Exodus 34:5–7, God shares His heart and nature with Moses with these words. "The Lord God, merciful and gracious, longsuffering and abundant in goodness and truth. Keeping mercy for thousands, forgiving iniquity and transgressions and sin, and that will by no means clear the guilty." God desperately wants to forgive your sin and heal your life but can't do so if you do not bring your sin to Him.

As a father myself, I know of that kind of heart desire toward your children. My son was five years old when this happened. We had returned from Sunday morning church where I had received a report that John had had a bad day in children's church. I had chosen to wait until we were home to deal with it. I administered the standard three swats of corrective love after explaining the reason for it. After a spanking, I always offer my open arms to reaffirm my unconditional acceptance and love toward my child. This time, John would have nothing of it.

He ran the other way, down the hall into his bedroom, and would not show his face when called. As I called out my offer to give him a hug, he finally peeked out from his doorway. When he saw me waiting with open arms at the end of the hall, he darted back into hiding. We went through this scenario for over five minutes. Each time he would come out, move closer to the hug, but then retreat. Halfway down the hall, to the end of the hall, and finally to the fingers' edge of my outstretched arm, he came but would not step inside.

"Son, my arms are open wide, but you have to choose if you want the hug or not. I am not going to force you." After a long, hard moment, he leaps into my arm, and I hug him as if I would never let him go. We danced around the kitchen for several minutes in utter joy of the reunion. Tears were flowing down my eyes as I told him how much I loved him and how proud of him I was. It was a moment I will never forget.

That night during my devotions, God told me He allowed that to happen so I would understand how much He wants me to run into His arms when I need love and forgiveness. My joy at John coming to me was small compared to how He feels when I come to Him. Your sin is no problem to God. Not bringing your sin to God is the problem. Don't let stubborn pride and fear keep you from such an experience with God.

Application

Take some time and think about some failures in your life. Ask God to forgive you and to turn it into something that helps you or others in the future. Note the feeling of peace that comes when you give it over to God.

Now as an object lesson, take a piece of raw meat, place it on a paper plate, and leave it on the floorboard in the back seat of your car. In time, the smell will get bad and only worsen if you ignore it. The same is true of sin in your life. God wants to clean it, and He is the only one who can. Ignoring that fact will only produce a greater stench in your life.

12

Pugh proverb: "My responsibility is to obey; results is God's."

Scripture verses: 1 Samuel 15:22–23; Daniel 3:16–18; John 14:15; John 11:37–44; Luke 5:4–6

Though *obey* is a four-letter word, most people consider it a "four-letter word," meaning, it's a bad word. People are taught today to question authority before obeying. I know when I ask today's young people to do something, most of them ask to know why they should do it. Obedience is not their first thought. They want to know why so they can decide if it meets with their approval. They believe obedience is not right in and of itself.

I understand that in this evil world, there are occasions where what you are being asked to do should be evaluated before obeying, but God's commands do not fall into that category. He always has our good in mind. I am very thankful I learned this truth by growing up in a loving but obedience-driven Christian home. We were expected to obey simply because obedience to your parents and other authorities was right. If you obeyed, good things would happen.

It's like planting seeds. If you plant good seeds, good things will grow. The power to make things grow is in the seed. All you do is plant and take care of it. The miracle of growth is God designed. That's the way God made it to work. It's the same thing with obedience. God takes care of the results if we "plant" obedience.

Not only was my mother a part of teaching me this principle, my older brothers also played a part. When they began to teach me a sport such as baseball, they would always start with the fundamentals. "Keep your back elbow up. Spread your legs apart about the width of your shoulders. Look at the pitch all the way into the plate. Don't pull your head out." These and many more instructions were given to me. I didn't know why I should do these things and what would be the result of doing so. I just did it because I was told to. They promised good results if I would obey their instructions, and they were right.

Simon Peter learned this lesson of "just obey" in Luke 5:4–6. He and his fellow fishermen had been fishing all night and had caught nothing. Upon coming to shore, they encountered Jesus, who asked to teach from inside their boat. After he finished his teaching, Jesus told them to launch out a little way from the shore and cast out their nets. Peter explained the night's failures, but even though he thought it was a waste of time, he did as the Master had asked. His nets were immediately filled with so many fish, the nets began to break.

When they got the fish into the boat, there were so many, the boat began to sink. They had to get out of the boat to keep it afloat. Simon's part was to simply obey. He didn't have to know about the miraculous result that was about to take place. He just needed to do what Jesus had told him to do. When he did, God took over and did what God does—amazing things.

I have seen God do this in every area of my life. One area is that of witnessing to others about their need of Christ as their Savior. When I was young, I hated going witnessing. I was afraid I would do or say something wrong that would turn people away from Christ. When we would go into the jail to witness, I would pray no one would be in there, not for their benefit but mine.

The day I led my first person to Christ, God taught me another Pugh proverb. The only way to fail at witnessing is to fail to witness. He said if I would be faithful to obey and witness, He would do the rest. I reluctantly went into the jail that day and shared the gospel with a sixteen-year-old boy. To my wonder and amazement, he accepted Christ as his Lord and Savior. God's miracle of salvation which He did in that boy's heart that day was a beautiful thing of which to be a part. All I had to do was obey. God did the rest. Not every time I witness to someone do they get saved, but I am no longer afraid to do so. I am commanded to share the truth. What they do with it is between them and God.

Another example from my life concerns coaching the varsity boys' basketball team at the Christian school where I taught. I had determined to build my basketball team upon principles from the Bible. Hard work, working together as a team, understanding the game, and honoring God in all we do were the foundation of my coaching philosophy. The boys had bought into it and were working hard. However, it wasn't translating into wins. We had lost our first six games.

I sought God over the matter. I complained, "I am following your principles in what we are doing. Why aren't you blessing us?"

"You just keep obeying. I want you to start spending the first fifteen minutes of practice as a team in silent prayer and meditation," was His reply. Spending less time practicing when you are losing does not seem like a smart idea, but I obeyed, leaving the results up to God.

What He did was nothing short of a miracle. We went on a thirteen-game winning streak, winning both our conference and then the regional championship. The only thing we were doing different was what God had instructed us to do. Though we lost to the three-time state champions in overtime, it was an amazing season. We obeyed. God gave the results.

In Daniel 3:16–18, we read of three young men who understood the power of obedience. Shadrach, Meshach, and Abednego were required by King Nebuchadnezzar to bow down and worship a statue of the king as a sign of their allegiance. In doing so, they would be disobeying Jehovah God. If they did not, they would be thrown into a fiery furnace. Their answer to King Nebuchadnezzar shows they understood this Pugh proverb.

"We are not worried about how to answer you in this matter. If He wants to, our God whom we serve is able to deliver us from the burning fiery furnace, and he will deliver us out of your hand, O king. But if not, be it known unto thee, O king that we will not serve your gods, nor worship the golden image which you have set up" Daniel 3:16–18.

They knew their part was to obey. They trusted God's goodness in the outcome no matter what that meant. If you know the story, God did not deliver them out of the fiery furnace but was in it with them. He kept them from being burned or even having the smell of smoke upon them. Once again, God does amazing things when we first trust and obey Him.

God's Word says in John 14:15, "If you love me, keep my commandments." When you know God's character, you don't have to know what He is going to do, only that it will be good. You love Him because He first loved you. You trust Him because of that love. In the book of 1 John, it says that "perfect love casts out fear." That is why you need to focus on the details of your obedience, not the results.

Doing exactly what God says out of an obedient heart is vitally important. King Saul learned this in 1 Samuel 15. He was told to wait on the prophet Samuel to offer a sacrifice to God before going into battle with the Philistines. Samuel didn't come as quickly as Saul had anticipated. During that waiting period, Saul's army began to dwindle in size because of the wait. Saul panicked and offered the sacrifice himself. Shortly thereafter, Samuel showed up and chastised Saul with these words.

"Has the Lord as great delight in burnt offerings and sacrifices as in obeying His voice? Because to obey is better than sacrificing and to listen and do what I said than the fat of rams. For rebellion is the same as the sin of witchcraft and stubbornness is as iniquity and idolatry. Because you have rejected the word of the Lord, he has rejected you from being king" (1 Samuel 15:22–23). God didn't need a certain number of soldiers to give Saul the victory. He needed Saul's obedience.

One of the hardest lessons in getting people to obey and leave the results up to God is in the area of tithing. God's Word commands a person to give Him the first 10 percent of all income. Obviously, God doesn't need your money. This is a test to see if you trust in God as your provider or in money. People have said to me, "How can this work? I already can't pay my bills. How will giving away money help?"

"God makes promises to provide for those who honor him," is my standard response.

Until you have tried it and obeyed, it doesn't make sense. Once you make that leap of faith and just do it, you'll see God will provide. I have seen it work in my own life and have had hundreds of people over the years share with me the same results. God doesn't always do it in the same way, but He always meets the need.

I will give one more example from the Bible as I finish with this Pugh proverb. The story is found in John 11:37–44. Mary and Martha's brother Lazarus had died four days earlier and been sealed in a tomb. Jesus has arrived and just commanded them to roll the stone from in front of the tomb. Mary and Martha do not want to do that because the decaying body would have provided a terrible smell when the tomb was opened. Jesus challenges them that if they obey, they would behold the glory of God. Reluctantly, they obeyed.

Jesus calls out, "Lazarus, come forth." A form is seen in the shadows of the tomb, waddling out of the darkness because of the burial wrappings. It is Lazarus raised from the dead. Without Mary and Martha's obedience, Lazarus would have remained dead in the tomb. Many a miracle has laid dead in your life because you could not trust in God's goodness and simply obeyed, leaving the results up to God.

Application

By nature, I don't trust GPS guidance systems. A few times, they gave confusing directions and let me down. I am a get-there-by-landmarks kind of guy. My wife will make me place the address of a location in my phone when we're going somewhere that we're a little bit uncertain of how to get there.

If she doesn't like the way we are headed, she will defy the instructions of the GPS voice and go her own way. That drives me crazy. "Either trust the thing or don't use it," is what I usually say to her. Following the directions of the GPS has been of great benefit especially when we don't know where we are going.

Now, it is your turn. Pick an address in your area that you don't know how to get to. Put it into your phone's GPS system and follow the promptings of the voice. I'll bet you get there.

Unlike the GPS system, God never makes mistakes. Just follow His directions, and I bet you will end up right where you need to be.

13

Pugh proverb: "Choice does not determine the heart but reveals it."

Scripture verses: John 13:2, 21–30; 2 Timothy 4:10; Acts 5:1–11; Hebrews 11:4; Hebrews 11:24–26; Daniel 1:8; Revelation 22:11; Matthew 5:27–28

Does stealing make you a thief or were you already a thief and that's why you steal? Are people basically good but do bad things, or do the bad things they do reveal a sin nature within? I will answer this question from an experience in my own life.

I was five years old. Every Sunday, my mother would give me some money to put in the offering plate in my Sunday school class. Because I was young and the possibility of me losing it was high, it was usually a nickel or a dime. On this particular Sunday, it was a nickel, but not just any nickel. It was a buffalo head nickel. It had the engraving of a buffalo on one side and the head of a Native American on the other. It was really cool and now they are extremely rare.

I decided I wanted to keep such a cool nickel that Sunday and left it in my pocket when the offering plate was passed around the Sunday school class. The problem was, I forgot I had done that and left it in my pocket when we got home from church. When mom washed my clothes, she found the nickel and asked me why I hadn't given it to Jesus. I told her I planned to swap it out in the future for a nickel I would earn and then give it to Jesus.

I thought that was a pretty good line to keep me out of trouble. Mom wasn't buying it. She explained how I had dishonored God by stealing His money and I had lied to cover it up. She said I had a heart problem. My sinful Adamic nature had revealed itself, and that's why Jesus had to die on the cross. My sin, the sin of lying and stealing, had put Him on the cross. Then she spanked me until she was sure I would never be doing that again. I am glad she did. It was an act of love.

Judas Iscariot is an example of the same thing in the Bible (John 13:2, 21–30). He looked squeaky clean from the outside. He was one of the twelve disciples of Jesus. He had been following Him for three and a half years. No one suspected what was in his heart. No one, that is, but Jesus. The Scriptures say that Jesus from the beginning knew who would betray Him. Even at the Last Supper, the other disciples did not suspect Judas was about to betray Jesus Christ. When Jesus announced that one of them would betray Him, each disciple suspected themselves before they did Judas. His choice revealed his heart. It did not determine it.

The Bible is full of people who for a time appeared one way but really in their heart were another. Paul, in 2 Timothy 4:10 says, "Demas has forsaken me having loved this present world." Demas had been a helper in Paul's ministry at an earlier time, but evidently his heart had tainted motives in doing so. When the going got tough when Paul was thrown in prison, Demas showed his true colors. He loved the world more than God.

Hypocrites are found in every area of life, but it is especially disappointing when they are found in church. Acts 5:1–11 tells the story of two such people. Ananias and Sapphira were two people in the early church who found out the hard way the dangers of seemingly good choices coming out of a bad heart.

They had sold some land and had given a portion of it to the disciples to meet the financial needs of people in the community. By their actions, you would have thought they were generous, people-loving Christians with good hearts. If so, you would have been wrong. They lied about giving the entire sum of money because they wanted to be praised for their deed and appear humble and caring.

You can't fool God, and that was exactly what they were trying to do. God took it pretty personally and made an example of that kind of phony Christianity. They fell down dead after each affirmed to the apostles and God they had given their all. It cost them their all for such actions, their very lives.

Not all choices reveal evil hearts. Sometimes, the hardest choices reveal the best character. When I was a youth pastor at a church in North Carolina, our youth group was playing football in a field that was right beside someone's home.

One of the guys on my team was running a hitch-and-go move on the defender per my instructions. A hitch-and-go move is when the receiver stops as if it is a short pass and then pivots quickly and goes long.

The defender bit on the move and my receiver was in the clear. He was running toward the end zone. As the quarterback, I let a beauty of a pass fly from my hands. However, it wasn't as beautiful as I had hoped. In my excitement, I had thrown it a little long. My receiver was fast and made up the ground and made the catch.

The problem was the catch was right in front of a bush in the neighbor's yard. He plowed into it, doing no damage to himself but plenty to the bush. It knocked limbs and blossoms off about a quarter of the decorative plant. I was mortified. The neighbors had been cold and standoffish every time we had played at the field. I was scared, but I knew what I had to do—the right thing.

Because it was almost dark when it happened, I waited until the next day to face the music. I knocked on the door and waited. Two stern-looking faces greeted me at the door. I began my apology with a recounting of what had happened and an assurance of it never happening again. I finished with an offer to pay for any damages or any other punitive measures they might require.

Their response is something I will never forget. They started their comments by telling me they had not seen the damage until that morning. They had not seen who had done it but had suspected "those church young people." Hypocritical Christians had turned them away from going to church years earlier, so they had a very low opinion of "religious people."

However, my taking responsibility for my actions showed a different character. They had been watching us, and me in particular, for several months, trying to determine if we were genuine or not. My apology had solidified their belief that I was the real deal. They started attending church and became lifelong friends.

I have heard it said that character is what you are when no one is watching. I have asked teenagers at devotionals what they would be willing to do if they knew no one would find it out. That is the true test of who and what you are. Daniel was in that type of situation during his young life.

He and other young people had been taken captive by the Babylonians when they conquered Israel. They had been taken back to Babylon to be "retrained" for use in the Babylonian government. This retraining included dietary changes that would require them to disobey the laws of God. Daniel 1:8 says, "Daniel purposed in his heart that he would not make himself unacceptable before God by eating what the king had allotted for him to eat of the meat from the king's menu nor with the wine which the king himself drank."

It would have been easy for Daniel to justify compromising his standards. After all, he was in a foreign land not by his choice. The food and the choice was not his doing. To refuse the king's meat and drink would have been an insult to the king that could cost him his life. No one would blame him for the decision to do it.

Daniel knew he would cease to be who he was if he defied his conscience and his God. Daniel made the tough choices from his heart that God used to bring him to greatness. He served successfully under three different world rulers yet never compromised who he was. Even to his last days, he was willing to be thrown into a den of hungry lions rather than stop praying to Jehovah God. Choice did not determine his heart. It revealed it.

The quality of my marriage is tied to hard choices I made as a teenager. I had determined not to kiss a girl unless I was romantically in love with her. A kiss is a nonverbal way of saying, "I love you." On several occasions, that standard was put to the test. One such occasion was a party being held at my neighbor's house on a Saturday night. She was in the same class as me and had invited select girls and guys to come to the party. I was one of those privileged people.

Even though there would be several very attractive classmates there, I really didn't want to go. I suspected that the party would challenge my Christian standards, and I didn't want to put myself in that type of compromising situation. When I failed to arrive at the party, my neighbor sent her mother down to my house to beg me to come. Evidently, she and some of her friends were disappointed I wasn't there.

I gave in and headed across the yard to her house. The party was in full swing. They had been dancing but had stopped for some refreshments before beginning the next party game. I grabbed a soda and joined the group. I didn't know what the next game was. There was a circle of chairs with one chair in the middle with a blindfold on it. I was instructed to take a seat in one of the chairs in the circle. Each chair had a number taped on it.

I chose my favorite number, ten, and sat down, waiting for further instructions. Two bowls were brought out. The boys' chair numbers were placed into one bowl, and girls' chair numbers were put into the other. My neighbor closed her eyes and chose a number from the boys' bowl. Thank God it wasn't mine. He was instructed to sit in the chair in the middle and to put on the blindfold.

Next, a girl's number was picked. She was to silently get up, kiss the guy in the chair, and return to her seat. The guy was then instructed to take off the blindfold and guess who had kissed him. As long as he got it right, he got to continue being in the chair. If not, it was a girl's turn to sit in the seat and a boy kisser was chosen, and the game continued.

I had determined in my heart I was not going to violate my principles but did not know how to get out of the situation without it becoming embarrassing. I didn't want to be viewed as weird, nor did I want to come across as holier-than-thou by condemning them for their desire to kiss solely for their own pleasure. I began to earnestly pray. "Lord, get me out of here."

Just then, God allowed the soda I had drank earlier to kick in. There was a growing need in my bladder for some alone time. After the first round of kissing and before new numbers could be drawn, I announced my need of the restroom and headed toward my neighbor's bathroom. When finished, I determined not to go back to the party but to walk home.

When I arrived back at the house early, my mother asked me why I was back so early. I explained the situation. She was pleased by my decision and said those standards would pay off in the long run. I then decided I was going to go soak in the bathtub and try to feel better about the whole thing. It was a good thing too. After discovering I was not at her house anymore, my neighbor sent her mother back to my house to see what was going on.

My mother told the truth without going into too many details. She said I was taking a hot bath in order to feel better. That was enough to satisfy my neighbor's mother, and she left. On Monday, no one questioned me concerning why I had left, only that they had missed me. Thank God! I guess they thought I had gone to the bathroom because I wasn't feeling good and that was why I left. God is good.

I have a wonderful love relationship with my wife. It is deeply satisfying on all levels. I can honestly say I still get a thrill when I kiss her. It means something and is just not a chemical urge. My tough choice revealed a heart that understood the value and purpose of human touch. It did not determine it.

Moses had the same hard choices that I had made when he was growing up in Egypt as the adopted son of Pharaoh's sister. Hebrews 11:24–26 records, "By faith Moses, when he had become an adult, refused to be called the son of Pharaoh's daughter; Choosing rather to suffer afflictions with the people of God, than to enjoy the pleasures of sin for a season; counting the reproach of Christ greater riches than the treasures in Egypt: for he knew the lasting value of God's reward."

Moses is in God's hall of fame of faith because he had lived in a worldly environment and found it to be wanting in lasting satisfaction and purpose. His heart wanted more than this shallow world could give him. Moses's choice did not make the man but the man made the choice.

I will end this proverb and the book with a last example of the choice revealing the heart and not determining it. Hebrews 11:4

sums up the story of Cain and Abel this way. "By faith Abel offered unto God a more excellent sacrifice than Cain, by which he obtained witness that he was righteous, God testifying of his gifts: and by his story, he being dead still speaks." God already knows who will trust In Jesus for salvation. Time, and more specifically, your life exists so you can see what God already knows: the condition of your heart.

The Bible declares we all were born with a sinful heart because of Adam and Eve's choice to allow sin into the world. You don't have to teach a child to disobey. He must learn the art of obedience. Your choices do not make you a sinner. They reveal to you your sin problem before God. It is a heart issue.

Good works as an attempt to take away your sins only reveals a heart full of pride and self-righteousness. You reject God's gift of salvation because you have a rebellious soul. Only by admitting you are a hopeless, helpless sinner in need of a Savior can you make the choice to accept the payment of Christ's death and resurrection for your salvation.

My good deeds are done not to obtain salvation for me but are the evidence of a changed heart through the miracle of new birth as described in John 3:16–17. They reveal a soul made righteous through the blood of Jesus Christ. Both Cain and Abel appeared before God, but Cain's offering revealed the pride of his heart while Abel's revealed a heart depending on the sacrifice of the lamb.

Choice does not determine the heart but reveals it. What is the condition of your heart if you were to stand before God today? Someday that time will come. I pray this and the other Pugh proverbs have prepared you for that day.

Application

I want you to administer a survey of at least ten questions for this application. The survey consists of examples of choices people make. You will be asking this question to those who participate in your survey: "What does this tell you about the person?" You can make up your own list or you can use this one I give you as an example.

1. If someone looks at a pornographic website, what does that tell you about that person?
2. If a person watches cooking shows all the time, what does that tell you about that person?
3. If a person subscribes to a monthly golf magazine, what does it tell you about the person?
4. If someone helps a little old lady cross the street, what does it tell you about the person?
5. A person is wearing a big American flag on their shirt. What does it tell you about that person?
6. If a person goes regularly to church, what does that tell you about them?
7. If a person is a schoolteacher, what does it tell you about that person?
8. If a person is a librarian, what does that tell you about them?
9. If a person drives a sports car, what does that tell you about that person?
10. If a person goes regularly to the opera, what does that tell you about them?

One's choice does not determine their heart but reveals it.

About the Author

Dr. Dwane Pugh was born in North Carolina in 1958. He came to know Christ as his personal Savior at the age of eight. Three years later, he felt the call of God to go into full-time Christian ministry. Since then, God has been working on Dwane to conform him into a tool fit for the Master's use. Dwane received a bachelor's degree in theology from Piedmont Bible College in Winston Salem, North Carolina. He also attended Liberty University and North Carolina School of Theology to get his master's and doctorate degrees in theology.

Through the years, God has allowed Dwane to serve Him in a variety of ministries. He has traveled with puppet ministries, singing groups, and mission teams in two different countries. Dwane has been the assistant pastor, music and youth director at two different churches, was the director of a family center ministry, and has taught in Christian schools. God has allowed Dwane to direct and speak at youth camps and conferences across the eastern seaboard.

Sports has also been a part of the ministry God has used Dwane to do. He coached a USA soccer team for two years at the Youth World Cup in Gothenburg, Sweden, and has coached the local high school team for twenty-three years. Dwane regularly puts on sports camps in a variety of sports in order to share the gospel.

CPSIA information can be obtained
at www.ICGtesting.com
Printed in the USA
BVHW081750110122
625982BV00007BA/178